THE STATE OF THE U.S.A. ATLAS

THE STATE OF THE U.S.A. ATLAS

The Changing Face of American Life
in Maps and Graphics

Doug Henwood

A TOUCHSTONE BOOK
Published by Simon & Schuster Inc.
New York   London   Toronto   Sydney   Tokyo   Singapore

45130150

ㅈ☰

SIMON & SCHUSTER/TOUCHSTONE
Rockefeller Center
1230 Avenue of the Americas
New York, New York 10020

Published in Great Britain by
Penguin Books, London

Edited and co-ordinated for Myriad Editions by Anne Benewick
with Dorothy Green

Design by Corinne Pearlman

Maps created by David McCutcheon for
Swanston Publishing Limited, Derby, England

Printed and bound in Hong Kong
Produced by Mandarin Offset Ltd.

10 9 8 7 6 5 4 3 2 1 ppb
10 9 8 7 6 5 4 3 2 1 hc

Library of Congress Cataloging-in-Publication Data

Henwood, Doug.
   The state of the U.S.A. atlas: the changing face of American life
in maps and graphics / Doug Henwood.
        p.   cm.
"A touchstone book."
Contents: Demographics — Economy — Society — Government.
ISBN 0-671-79696-8. — ISBN 0-671-79695-X (pbk.)
   1. United States—Maps.   2. United States—Social conditions—
Maps.   3. United States—Economic conditions—Maps.   I. Title.
II. Title: State of the United States of America atlas.
G1200.H45   1994 <G&M>
912. 73—dc20

                                                            94-14142
                                                                CIP
                                                                MAP

Figures on religious identification used on pages 72–73 are from
One Nation Under God by Barry A. Kosmin and Seymour P. Lachman.
Reprinted by permission of Crown Publishers Inc.

CONTENTS

INTRODUCTION

If any generalization can be made from the material covered in this atlas, it's that American society contains within it tremendous contradictions. The U.S. is the richest country the world has ever seen, but it has a poverty rate unmatched among its industrial peers. Americans think of themselves as the nation where everyone is middle class, but the U.S. has the smallest middle class among that same set of nations. It spends more on health than any other country in the world, but some of its health statistics are worse than any in the northern hemisphere. Abortion is supposedly legal, but in practice it's unavailable to millions of women. American universities are among the best in the world, but basic education and literacy are neglected. Americans think of their democracy as a model for others to follow, yet half the population doesn't bother to vote. I could go on, but this book can do the work for me.

A few points should be kept in mind while turning these pages, but perhaps most important is that this atlas is built from social statistics that are really only approximations of reality, not reality itself.

People and societies are unlike, say, atoms in a jar, which can be trusted to behave in similar ways across time and space. Most social statistics are built on surveys – asking people questions about their behavior or opinions which they may or may not answer truthfully. Most surveys only canvass a small portion of the population, and extrapolate from those answers to the entire society; 10,000 or 60,000 people are selected as stand-ins for a quarter-billion. Even the best survey can't be sure that it's picked a representative sample of people, and those missed are often those at the extremes of society, the poor and rich, who are in many ways the most interesting to study. Even the Census taken every ten years, which is supposed to cover every household in the country, makes huge mistakes; it's estimated (on the basis of *another* survey) that the 1990 effort made as many as 25 million errors, such as double-counting, counting people in the wrong place, and counting the non-existent and the dead.

That's not to say the whole enterprise is worthless, or that Census-takers are liars or incompetents. Quite the contrary – over the years, I've been impressed with the honesty, professionalism, and openness of U.S. government statisticians. Almost without exception, they're happy to share their data with journalists and the public and to discuss its virtues and shortcomings. The information they do collect and publish is rich in detail, and essential to any understanding of American society. But it isn't perfect, and it's subject to divergent interpretations and definitions. Look, for example, at the wide variations in the poverty rate, given in **18. The Promised Land**, that depend on your definition of penury. Issues like this are thrashed over in the notes.

A cautionary note on language is also necessary. Throughout this atlas, terms like "black," "Hispanic," and "minority" are used, all of which have their problems. Many people, for example, don't like the word "Hispanic," either preferring "Latino" or objecting to the use of a single term to cover a very diverse population. Many "Hispanics" consider themselves "white," and are offended by the concept of "non-Hispanic white." We've tried to convey some of these complexities in the graphics and the notes to the maps, but the results probably won't please everyone. More broadly, presenting the social gaps among regions, ethnic groups, and social classes is often condemned as negative and divisive. But it serves no purpose but apologetics to ignore those divisions. The point of this book is to show America as it really is, not as I'd like it to be – peaceful, egalitarian, and democratic.

Many thank yous are in order. Not only government statisticians, but private researchers and academics were all highly cooperative; for all its problems, this is a very open society. Kimberly Phillips gathered much of the raw material for this book, and did it with great intelligence and persistence; I can't imagine what I'd have done without her help. Michael Tremonte put out some threatening data fires as the deadline approached. Major thanks are also owed to Anne Benewick and her colleagues at Myriad Editions, who transformed deadly columns of figures into the snazzy graphics that follow. Anne is really the co-author of this book even though her name appears nowhere on the cover. The designer, Corinne Pearlman, did a marvelous job of turning ideas into computer images, and David McCutcheon worked hard on putting together the final artwork. Thanks also to my agent, Phil Pochoda, who both delivered this project to me and helped plan its evolution. And finally, thanks to my wife, Christine Bratton, who displayed great patience while her husband was temporarily transformed into Map Man; life would be inconceivable without her.

Doug Henwood
New York, April 1994

Russian 1.2%
Norwegian 1.6%
Swedish 1.9%

Scottish 2.2%
Scotch-Irish 2.3%
Dutch 2.5%

American Indian 3.5%
Polish 3.8%

French 4.1%
Mexican 4.7%

American 5%
Italian 5.9%

Afro American 9.6%

English 13.1%

Irish 15.6%

German 23.3%

Ancestry of Americans as
declared in the 1990 Census
*all groups representing more
than one percent of the population*

ALASKA

WASHINGTON

OREGON

IDAHO

MONTANA

NORTH DAKOTA

MINNESOTA

WYOMING

SOUTH DAKOTA

WISCONSIN

M I C H I G A N

NEVADA

UTAH

IOWA

CALIFORNIA

COLORADO

NEBRASKA

ILLINOIS

INDIANA

OHIO

PEN

HAWAII

ARIZONA

KANSAS

MISSOURI

TENNESSEE

WEST VIRGINIA

KENTUCKY

ARKANSAS

NEW
MEXICO

OKLAHOMA

MISSISSIPPI

ALABAMA

GEORGIA

LOUISIANA

TEXAS

FLORI

1993   2020

1993 2020

1993   2020

1993 2020

SENIOR CITIZENS IN
THE U.S.POPULATION
1993 and 2020 *(projected)*
percentages
Source: U.S. Bureau of the Census

6.6   7.7%   0.9% 1.4%
women 65 - 84   women over 85

4.7%   6.6%   0.4% 0.7%
men 65 - 84   men over 85

For over 200 years the U.S. population has been moving southward and westward. At the end of the 20th century it is also getting older.

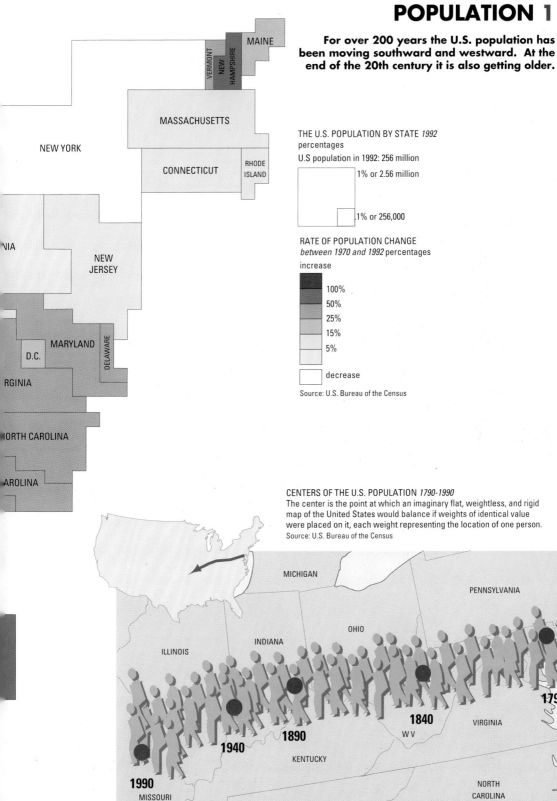

THE U.S. POPULATION BY STATE *1992*
percentages
U.S population in 1992: 256 million

1% or 2.56 million

.1% or 256,000

RATE OF POPULATION CHANGE
between 1970 and 1992 percentages
increase

100%
50%
25%
15%
5%

decrease

Source: U.S. Bureau of the Census

MAINE

VERMONT
NEW HAMPSHIRE

MASSACHUSETTS

NEW YORK

CONNECTICUT

RHODE ISLAND

NIA

NEW JERSEY

MARYLAND

D.C.

DELAWARE

RGINIA

ORTH CAROLINA

AROLINA

CENTERS OF THE U.S. POPULATION *1790-1990*
The center is the point at which an imaginary flat, weightless, and rigid map of the United States would balance if weights of identical value were placed on it, each weight representing the location of one person.
Source: U.S. Bureau of the Census

MICHIGAN

PENNSYLVANIA

OHIO

INDIANA

ILLINOIS

MD

1790

1840
W V

VIRGINIA

1890

1940

KENTUCKY

1990

MISSOURI

NORTH CAROLINA

TENNESSEE

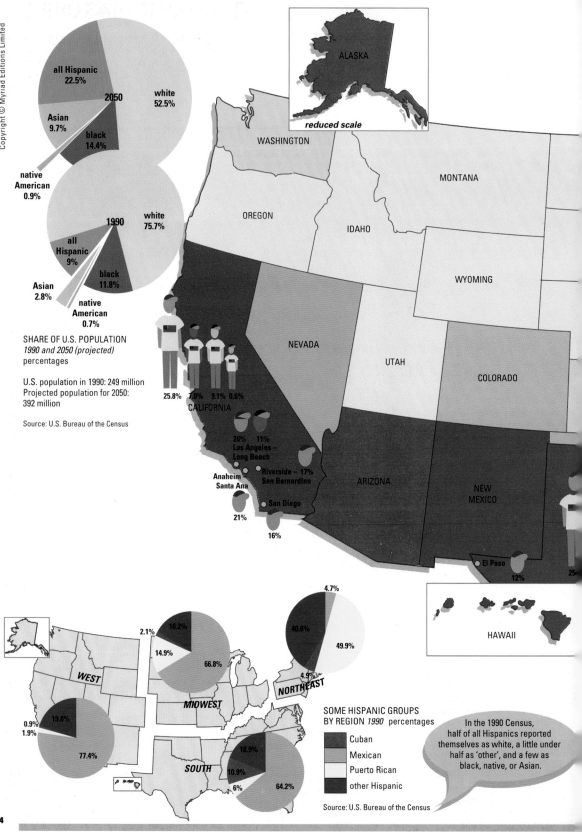

Copyright © Myriad Editions Limited

all Hispanic 22.5%
2050
white 52.5%
Asian 9.7%
black 14.4%
native American 0.9%

white 75.7%
1990
all Hispanic 9%
black 11.8%
Asian 2.8%
native American 0.7%

SHARE OF U.S. POPULATION
1990 and 2050 (projected)
percentages

U.S. population in 1990: 249 million
Projected population for 2050:
392 million

Source: U.S. Bureau of the Census

ALASKA
reduced scale

WASHINGTON
OREGON
IDAHO
MONTANA
WYOMING
NEVADA
UTAH
COLORADO
CALIFORNIA
ARIZONA
NEW MEXICO

25.8% 7.0% 9.1% 0.6%

26% 11%
Los Angeles –
Long Beach
Anaheim
Santa Ana
Riverside – 17%
San Bernardino
San Diego
21%
16%

El Paso
12%
25%

HAWAII

2.1% 16.2%
14.9%
66.8%

4.7%
40.6%
49.9%
4.9%

WEST
0.9%
1.9%
19.8%
77.4%

MIDWEST
NORTHEAST

SOUTH
18.9%
10.9%
6%
64.2%

SOME HISPANIC GROUPS
BY REGION *1990* percentages

- Cuban
- Mexican
- Puerto Rican
- other Hispanic

In the 1990 Census,
half of all Hispanics reported
themselves as white, a little under
half as 'other', and a few as
black, native, or Asian.

Source: U.S. Bureau of the Census

Race in America is no longer a matter of black and white. As complexity grows, both categories and language become more inadequate.

The Asian population in the U.S. doubled between 1980 and 1990, led by Chinese, Indians, Filipinos and Koreans.

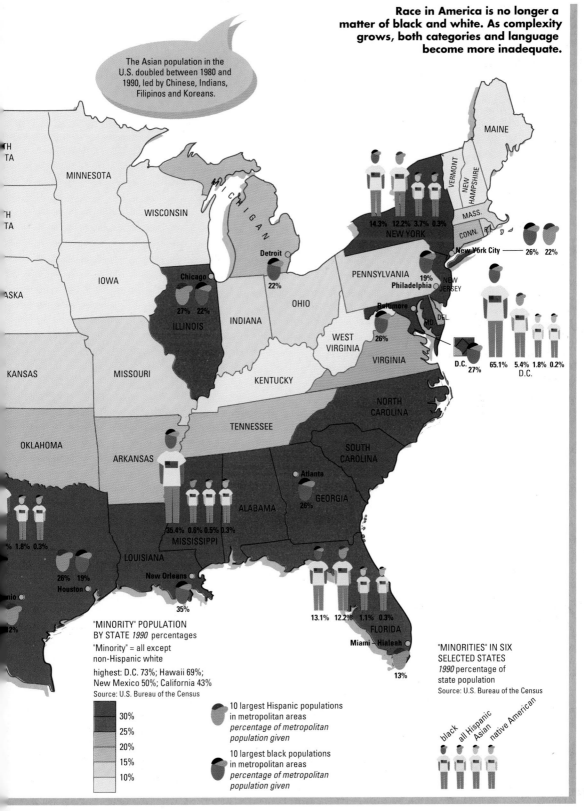

MAINE

MINNESOTA

WISCONSIN

MICHIGAN

VERMONT
NEW HAMPSHIRE
MASS.
CONN.

14.3% 12.2% 3.7% 0.3%
NEW YORK

New York City — 26% 22%

Detroit
22%

Chicago
27% 22%
ILLINOIS

IOWA

INDIANA

OHIO

PENNSYLVANIA
Philadelphia 19%
NEW JERSEY

Baltimore
MD.
DEL.

WEST VIRGINIA
26%

VIRGINIA

D.C.
27%

65.1% 5.4% 1.8% 0.2%
D.C.

KANSAS

MISSOURI

KENTUCKY

NORTH CAROLINA

OKLAHOMA

ARKANSAS

TENNESSEE

SOUTH CAROLINA

Atlanta

GEORGIA
26%

ALABAMA

35.4% 0.6% 0.5% 0.3%
MISSISSIPPI

LOUISIANA

New Orleans

26% 19%
Houston

...nio

...% 1.8% 0.3%

...2%

35%

13.1% 12.2% 1.1% 0.3%
FLORIDA

Miami – Hialeah

13%

"MINORITY" POPULATION BY STATE *1990* percentages
"Minority" = all except non-Hispanic white

highest: D.C. 73%; Hawaii 69%; New Mexico 50%; California 43%
Source: U.S. Bureau of the Census

30%
25%
20%
15%
10%

10 largest Hispanic populations in metropolitan areas
percentage of metropolitan population given

10 largest black populations in metropolitan areas
percentage of metropolitan population given

"MINORITIES" IN SIX SELECTED STATES
1990 percentage of state population
Source: U.S. Bureau of the Census

black   all Hispanic   Asian   native American

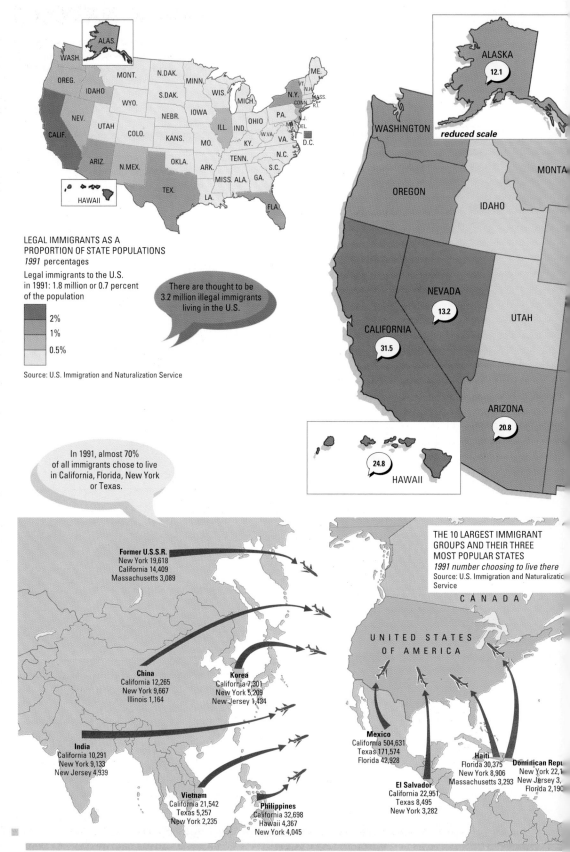

LEGAL IMMIGRANTS AS A PROPORTION OF STATE POPULATIONS
1991 percentages

Legal immigrants to the U.S.
in 1991: 1.8 million or 0.7 percent
of the population

- 2%
- 1%
- 0.5%

Source: U.S. Immigration and Naturalization Service

There are thought to be
3.2 million illegal immigrants
living in the U.S.

reduced scale

ALASKA
12.1

WASHINGTON

MONTA

OREGON

IDAHO

NEVADA
13.2

UTAH

CALIFORNIA
31.5

ARIZONA
20.8

24.8

HAWAII

In 1991, almost 70%
of all immigrants chose to live
in California, Florida, New York
or Texas.

Former U.S.S.R.
New York 19,618
California 14,409
Massachusetts 3,089

China
California 12,265
New York 9,667
Illinois 1,164

Korea
California 7,301
New York 5,209
New Jersey 1,434

India
California 10,291
New York 9,133
New Jersey 4,939

Vietnam
California 21,542
Texas 5,257
New York 2,235

Philippines
California 32,698
Hawaii 4,367
New York 4,045

THE 10 LARGEST IMMIGRANT GROUPS AND THEIR THREE MOST POPULAR STATES
1991 number choosing to live there
Source: U.S. Immigration and Naturalizatic
Service

C A N A D A

U N I T E D   S T A T E S
O F   A M E R I C A

Mexico
California 504,631
Texas 171,574
Florida 42,928

Haiti
Florida 30,375
New York 8,906
Massachusetts 3,293

Dominican Repu
New York 22,1
New Jersey 3,
Florida 2,190

El Salvador
California 22,951
Texas 8,495
New York 3,282

16

People from Asia and other parts of the Americas have replaced Europeans as the prominent newcomers.

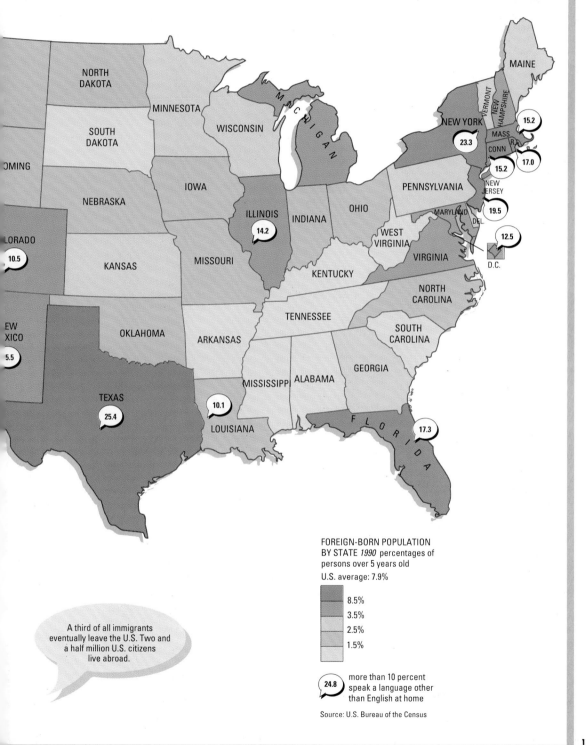

NORTH DAKOTA

MINNESOTA

SOUTH DAKOTA

WYOMING

NEBRASKA

IOWA

WISCONSIN

MICHIGAN

MAINE

VERMONT

NEW HAMPSHIRE

15.2

NEW YORK
23.3

MASS
R.I.
CONN
15.2   17.0

PENNSYLVANIA

NEW JERSEY
19.5

OHIO

INDIANA

ILLINOIS
14.2

MARYLAND
DEL.

WEST VIRGINIA

VIRGINIA

12.5

D.C.

COLORADO
10.5

KANSAS

MISSOURI

KENTUCKY

NORTH CAROLINA

NEW MEXICO
5.5

OKLAHOMA

ARKANSAS

TENNESSEE

SOUTH CAROLINA

TEXAS
25.4

LOUISIANA
10.1

MISSISSIPPI   ALABAMA

GEORGIA

FLORIDA
17.3

A third of all immigrants eventually leave the U.S. Two and a half million U.S. citizens live abroad.

FOREIGN-BORN POPULATION BY STATE *1990* percentages of persons over 5 years old

U.S. average: 7.9%

- 8.5%
- 3.5%
- 2.5%
- 1.5%

24.8 more than 10 percent speak a language other than English at home

Source: U.S. Bureau of the Census

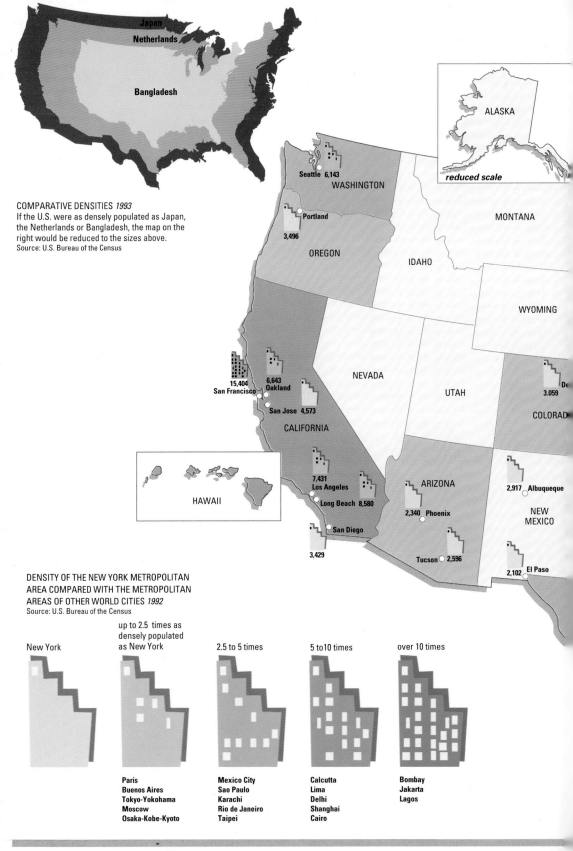

Copyright © Myriad Editions Limited

COMPARATIVE DENSITIES *1993*
If the U.S. were as densely populated as Japan,
the Netherlands or Bangladesh, the map on the
right would be reduced to the sizes above.
Source: U.S. Bureau of the Census

Japan
Netherlands
Bangladesh

ALASKA
reduced scale

Seattle 6,143
WASHINGTON

Portland
3,496
OREGON

MONTANA

IDAHO

WYOMING

15,404
San Francisco

6,643
Oakland

San Jose 4,573
CALIFORNIA

NEVADA

UTAH

De
3.059

COLORAD

7,431
Los Angeles

Long Beach 8,580

San Diego
3,429

HAWAII

ARIZONA

2,340 Phoenix

Tucson 2,596

2,917 Albuqueque

NEW
MEXICO

2,102 El Paso

**DENSITY OF THE NEW YORK METROPOLITAN
AREA COMPARED WITH THE METROPOLITAN
AREAS OF OTHER WORLD CITIES** *1992*
Source: U.S. Bureau of the Census

New York	up to 2.5 times as densely populated as New York	2.5 to 5 times	5 to10 times	over 10 times
	Paris	Mexico City	Calcutta	Bombay
	Buenos Aires	Sao Paulo	Lima	Jakarta
	Tokyo-Yokohama	Karachi	Delhi	Lagos
	Moscow	Rio de Janeiro	Shanghai	
	Osaka-Kobe-Kyoto	Taipei	Cairo	

ELBOW ROOM 4

Outside the Northeast, Americans enjoy a roominess experienced in few countries.

If the New York metropolitan area were as densely populated as Lagos, it could accommodate three quarters of the U.S. population.

MAINE

NORTH DAKOTA

MINNESOTA

SOUTH DAKOTA

WISCONSIN

MICHIGAN

VERMONT

NEW HAMPSHIRE

MASS.
Boston 11,958

NEW YORK

CONN.

R.I.

23,699 New York

6,542 Milwaukee

Detroit

7,396

IOWA

Chicago

Cleveland 6,607

PENNSYLVANIA

Pittsburgh

Philadelphia

NEW JERSEY

11,748

NEBRASKA

12,264

ILLINOIS

OHIO 6,571

2,022

Columbus

Indianapolis

INDIANA

Baltimore

9,086

DEL.

MARYLAND

1,394 Kansas City

MISSOURI

3,314

WEST VIRGINIA

1,585 Virginia Beach

D.C. 9,951

KANSAS

St. Louis

KENTUCKY

VIRGINIA

6,403

NORTH CAROLINA

Nashville-Davidson

2,276 Charlotte

2,383 Memphis

1,018

TENNESSEE

732 Oklahoma City

OKLAHOMA

ARKANSAS

SOUTH CAROLINA

Atlanta

MISSISSIPPI ALABAMA

GEORGIA

2,985

1,594 Fort Worth

Dallas

2,944

LOUISIANA

Jacksonville

TEXAS

2,138 Austin

3,020 Houston

New 2,746 Orleans

870

FLORIDA

San Antonio

2,811

PEOPLE PER SQUARE MILE
1990 numbers

U.S. average: 70 people per square mile

- 500
- 250
- 50
- 25
- 5

DENSITY IN THE CITIES
1990 40 largest U.S. cities

over 10,000 people per square mile
numbers given

5,000-10,000

below 5,000

Source: U.S. Bureau of the Census

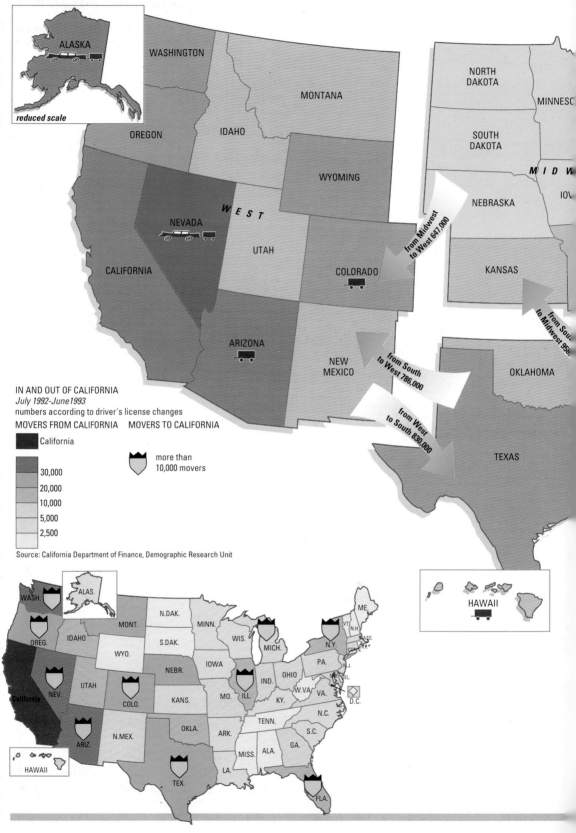

Copyright © Myriad Editions Limited

ALASKA
reduced scale

WASHINGTON

OREGON

IDAHO

MONTANA

WYOMING

NORTH DAKOTA

SOUTH DAKOTA

M I D W

NEBRASKA

IOV

W E S T

NEVADA

UTAH

CALIFORNIA

ARIZONA

COLORADO

NEW MEXICO

KANSAS

OKLAHOMA

TEXAS

MINNESO

from Midwest to West 647,000

from Sou to Midwest 95

from South to West 786,000

from West to South 830,000

IN AND OUT OF CALIFORNIA
July 1992-June 1993
numbers according to driver's license changes

MOVERS FROM CALIFORNIA   MOVERS TO CALIFORNIA

California

30,000
20,000
10,000
5,000
2,500

more than
10,000 movers

Source: California Department of Finance, Demographic Research Unit

HAWAII

WASH.

ALAS.

ME.

OREG.

IDAHO

MONT.

N.DAK.

MINN.

WIS.

MICH.

N.Y.

VT.
N.H.
MASS.
CONN. R.I.

California

NEV.

UTAH

WYO.

S.DAK.

NEBR.

IOWA

IND.

OHIO

PA.

N.J.
DEL.

COLO.

KANS.

MO.

ILL.

KY.

W.VA

VA.

D.C.

ARIZ.

N.MEX.

OKLA.

ARK.

TENN.

N.C.

S.C.

HAWAII

TEX.

LA.

MISS.

ALA.

GA.

FLA.

Americans move more often than most other people in the world.

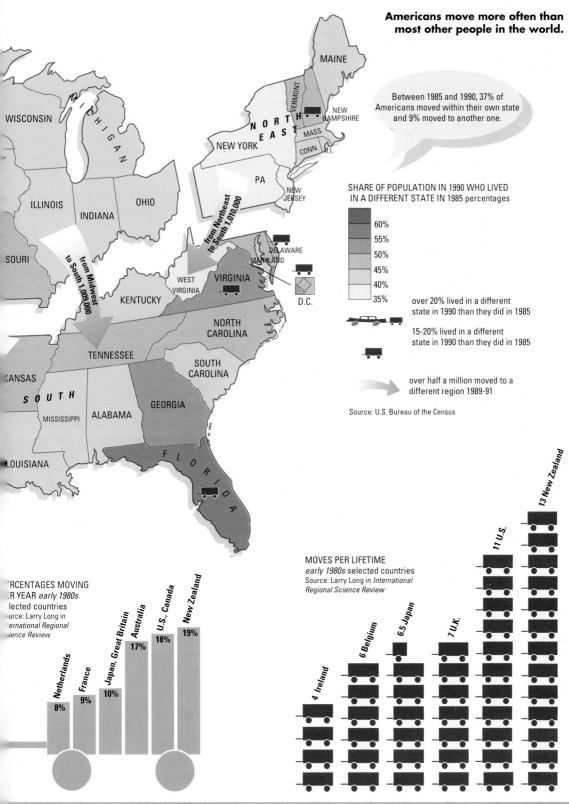

MAINE

VERMONT

NEW HAMPSHIRE

NORTH EAST

MASS.

NEW YORK

CONN. R.I.

PA

NEW JERSEY

WISCONSIN

MICHIGAN

ILLINOIS

INDIANA

OHIO

SOURI

from Northeast to South 1,010,000

from Midwest to South 1,009,000

DELAWARE

MARYLAND

WEST VIRGINIA

VIRGINIA

D.C.

KENTUCKY

NORTH CAROLINA

TENNESSEE

SOUTH CAROLINA

ANSAS

SOUTH

GEORGIA

MISSISSIPPI

ALABAMA

LOUISIANA

FLORIDA

Between 1985 and 1990, 37% of Americans moved within their own state and 9% moved to another one.

SHARE OF POPULATION IN 1990 WHO LIVED IN A DIFFERENT STATE IN 1985 percentages

- 60%
- 55%
- 50%
- 45%
- 40%
- 35%

over 20% lived in a different state in 1990 than they did in 1985

15-20% lived in a different state in 1990 than they did in 1985

over half a million moved to a different region 1989-91

Source: U.S. Bureau of the Census

PERCENTAGES MOVING PER YEAR *early 1980s* selected countries
Source: Larry Long in *International Regional Science Review*

- Netherlands 8%
- France 9%
- Japan, Great Britain 10%
- Australia 17%
- U.S., Canada 18%
- New Zealand 19%

MOVES PER LIFETIME
early 1980s selected countries
Source: Larry Long in *International Regional Science Review*

- 4 Ireland
- 6 Belgium
- 6.5 Japan
- 7 U.K.
- 11 U.S.
- 13 New Zealand

21

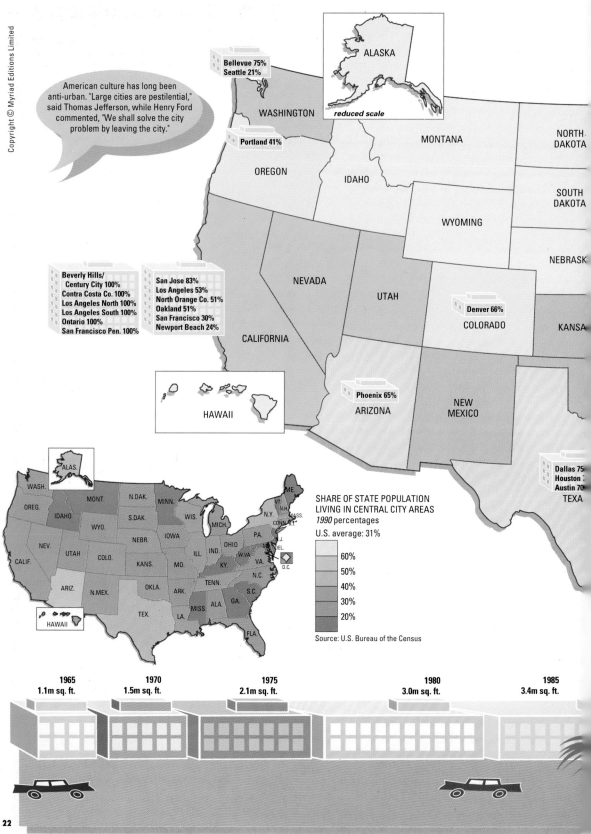

American culture has long been anti-urban. "Large cities are pestilential," said Thomas Jefferson, while Henry Ford commented, "We shall solve the city problem by leaving the city."

Bellevue 75%
Seattle 21%

Portland 41%

WASHINGTON

OREGON

IDAHO

MONTANA

WYOMING

NORTH DAKOTA

SOUTH DAKOTA

NEBRASK

ALASKA
reduced scale

Beverly Hills/
  Century City 100%
Contra Costa Co. 100%
Los Angeles North 100%
Los Angeles South 100%
Ontario 100%
San Francisco Pen. 100%

San Jose 83%
Los Angeles 53%
North Orange Co. 51%
Oakland 51%
San Francisco 30%
Newport Beach 24%

Denver 66%

NEVADA

UTAH

COLORADO

KANSA

CALIFORNIA

HAWAII

Phoenix 65%

ARIZONA

NEW MEXICO

Dallas 75
Houston
Austin 70

TEXAS

SHARE OF STATE POPULATION
LIVING IN CENTRAL CITY AREAS
1990 percentages
U.S. average: 31%

60%
50%
40%
30%
20%

Source: U.S. Bureau of the Census

1965	1970	1975	1980	1985
1.1m sq. ft.	1.5m sq. ft.	2.1m sq. ft.	3.0m sq. ft.	3.4m sq. ft.

Three-quarters of the population is urban,
but what Americans call cities probably
seem like suburbs to foreign eyes.

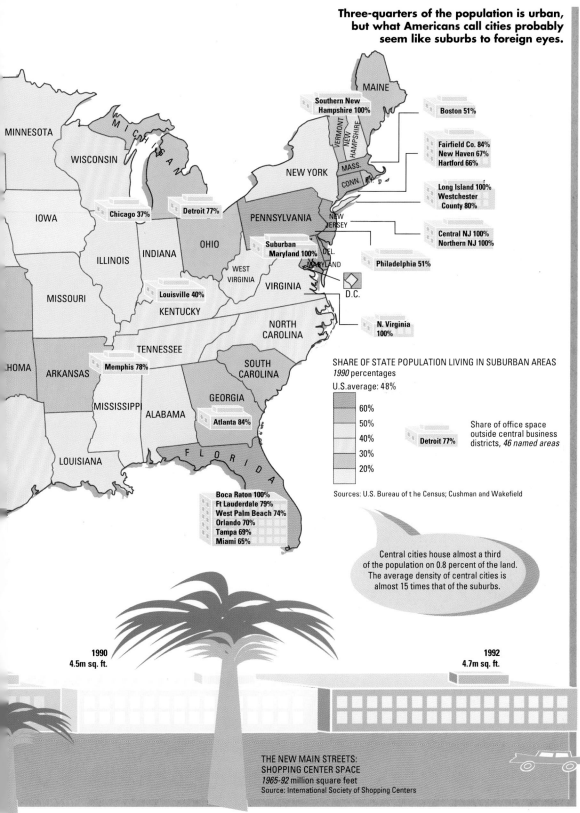

MAINE

Southern New
Hampshire 100%

Boston 51%

MINNESOTA

MICHIGAN

WISCONSIN

VERMONT

NEW
HAMPSHIRE

NEW YORK

MASS.

CONN.

Fairfield Co. 84%
New Haven 67%
Hartford 66%

Long Island 100%
Westchester
County 80%

IOWA

Chicago 37%

Detroit 77%

PENNSYLVANIA

NEW
JERSEY

Central NJ 100%
Northern NJ 100%

ILLINOIS

INDIANA

OHIO

Suburban
Maryland 100%

DEL.

Philadelphia 51%

WEST
VIRGINIA

MARYLAND

MISSOURI

Louisville 40%

VIRGINIA

D.C.

KENTUCKY

NORTH
CAROLINA

N. Virginia
100%

TENNESSEE

SHARE OF STATE POPULATION LIVING IN SUBURBAN AREAS
1990 percentages

U.S.average: 48%

OKLAHOMA

ARKANSAS

Memphis 78%

SOUTH
CAROLINA

GEORGIA

MISSISSIPPI

ALABAMA

Atlanta 84%

LOUISIANA

FLORIDA

	60%
	50%
	40%
	30%
	20%

Detroit 77%

Share of office space
outside central business
districts, *46 named areas*

Sources: U.S. Bureau of t he Census; Cushman and Wakefield

Boca Raton 100%
Ft Lauderdale 79%
West Palm Beach 74%
Orlando 70%
Tampa 69%
Miami 65%

Central cities house almost a third
of the population on 0.8 percent of the land.
The average density of central cities is
almost 15 times that of the suburbs.

1990
4.5m sq. ft.

1992
4.7m sq. ft.

THE NEW MAIN STREETS:
SHOPPING CENTER SPACE
1965-92 million square feet
Source: International Society of Shopping Centers

Part Two

ECONOMY

Per capita income
of Americans *1975-93*
calculated in 1987 U.S. dollars

$14,917	$16,584	$17,944	$19,593	$19,800
1975	1980	1985	1990	1993

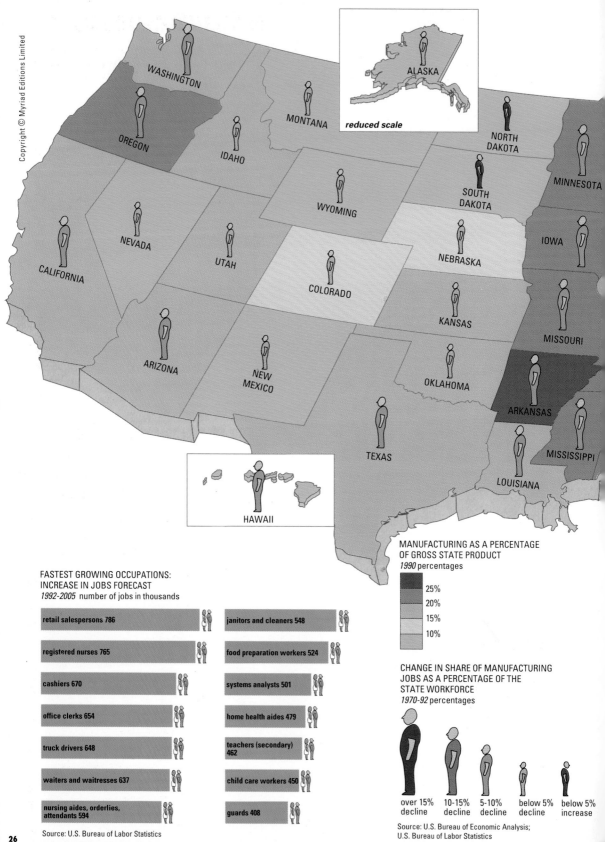

WASHINGTON

ALASKA

reduced scale

OREGON

MONTANA

NORTH DAKOTA

MINNESOTA

IDAHO

SOUTH DAKOTA

IOWA

NEVADA

WYOMING

CALIFORNIA

UTAH

NEBRASKA

COLORADO

KANSAS

MISSOURI

ARIZONA

NEW MEXICO

OKLAHOMA

ARKANSAS

MISSISSIPPI

TEXAS

LOUISIANA

HAWAII

MANUFACTURING AS A PERCENTAGE OF GROSS STATE PRODUCT
1990 percentages

- 25%
- 20%
- 15%
- 10%

FASTEST GROWING OCCUPATIONS: INCREASE IN JOBS FORECAST
1992-2005 number of jobs in thousands

retail salespersons 786	janitors and cleaners 548
registered nurses 765	food preparation workers 524
cashiers 670	systems analysts 501
office clerks 654	home health aides 479
truck drivers 648	teachers (secondary) 462
waiters and waitresses 637	child care workers 450
nursing aides, orderlies, attendants 594	guards 408

Source: U.S. Bureau of Labor Statistics

CHANGE IN SHARE OF MANUFACTURING JOBS AS A PERCENTAGE OF THE STATE WORKFORCE
1970-92 percentages

over 15% decline	10-15% decline	5-10% decline	below 5% decline	below 5% increase

Source: U.S. Bureau of Economic Analysis; U.S. Bureau of Labor Statistics

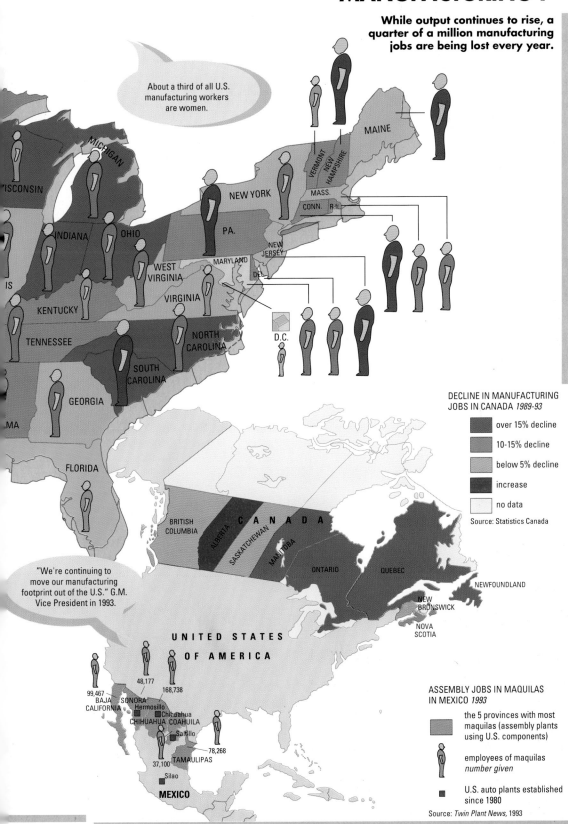

While output continues to rise, a quarter of a million manufacturing jobs are being lost every year.

About a third of all U.S. manufacturing workers are women.

MICHIGAN

WISCONSIN

MAINE

VERMONT

NEW HAMPSHIRE

NEW YORK

MASS.

CONN. R.I.

INDIANA   OHIO   PA.

NEW JERSEY

WEST VIRGINIA   MARYLAND

DEL.

VIRGINIA

KENTUCKY

D.C.

TENNESSEE   NORTH CAROLINA

SOUTH CAROLINA

GEORGIA

FLORIDA

"We're continuing to move our manufacturing footprint out of the U.S." G.M. Vice President in 1993.

DECLINE IN MANUFACTURING JOBS IN CANADA *1989-93*

- over 15% decline
- 10-15% decline
- below 5% decline
- increase
- no data

Source: Statistics Canada

BRITISH COLUMBIA   C A N A D A

ALBERTA   SASKATCHEWAN   MANITOBA

ONTARIO   QUEBEC

NEWFOUNDLAND

NEW BRUNSWICK

NOVA SCOTIA

UNITED STATES OF AMERICA

48,177

99,467   168,738

BAJA CALIFORNIA   SONORA   Hermosillo

Chihuahua

CHIHUAHUA   COAHUILA   Saltillo

78,268

37,100   TAMAULIPAS

Silao

MEXICO

ASSEMBLY JOBS IN MAQUILAS IN MEXICO *1993*

- the 5 provinces with most maquilas (assembly plants using U.S. components)
- employees of maquilas *number given*
- U.S. auto plants established since 1980

Source: *Twin Plant News*, 1993

U.S. SHARE OF WORLD FARM PRODUCTION AND EXPORTS
1992 percentages

production   exports

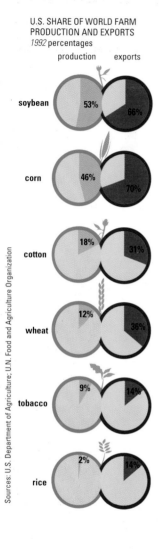

soybean   53%   66%

corn   46%   70%

cotton   18%   31%

wheat   12%   36%

tobacco   9%   14%

rice   2%   14%

Sources: U.S. Department of Agriculture; U.N. Food and Agriculture Organization

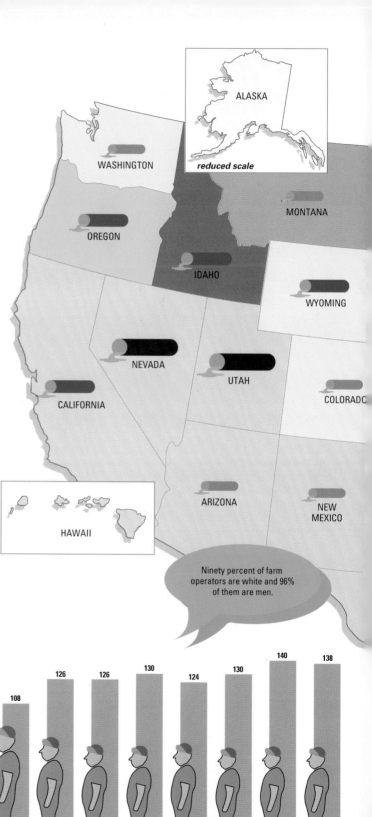

ALASKA

reduced scale

WASHINGTON

OREGON

MONTANA

IDAHO

WYOMING

NEVADA

UTAH

COLORADO

CALIFORNIA

HAWAII

ARIZONA

NEW MEXICO

Ninety percent of farm operators are white and 96% of them are men.

FARM OUTPUT AND EMPLOYMENT *1980-93*

index 1980=100

Sources: U.S. Department of Agriculture;
U.S. Bureau of Economic Analysis

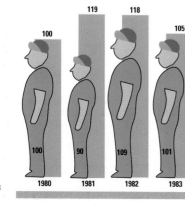

Year	Output	Employment
1980	100	100
1981	119	90
1982	118	109
1983	105	101
1984	108	92
1985	126	84
1986	126	79
1987	130	78
1988	124	80
1989	130	77
1990	140	78
1991	138	78

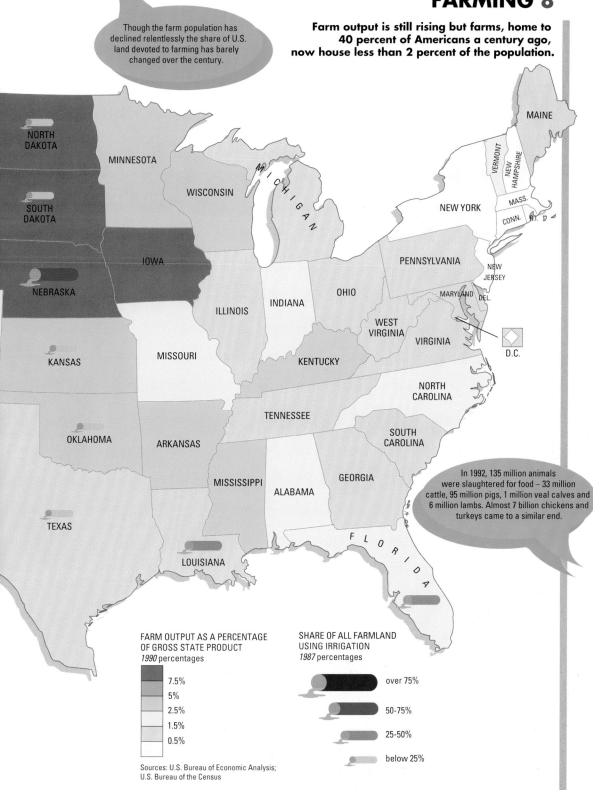

Though the farm population has declined relentlessly the share of U.S. land devoted to farming has barely changed over the century.

Farm output is still rising but farms, home to 40 percent of Americans a century ago, now house less than 2 percent of the population.

In 1992, 135 million animals were slaughtered for food – 33 million cattle, 95 million pigs, 1 million veal calves and 6 million lambs. Almost 7 billion chickens and turkeys came to a similar end.

FARM OUTPUT AS A PERCENTAGE OF GROSS STATE PRODUCT
1990 percentages

- 7.5%
- 5%
- 2.5%
- 1.5%
- 0.5%

SHARE OF ALL FARMLAND USING IRRIGATION
1987 percentages

- over 75%
- 50-75%
- 25-50%
- below 25%

Sources: U.S. Bureau of Economic Analysis; U.S. Bureau of the Census

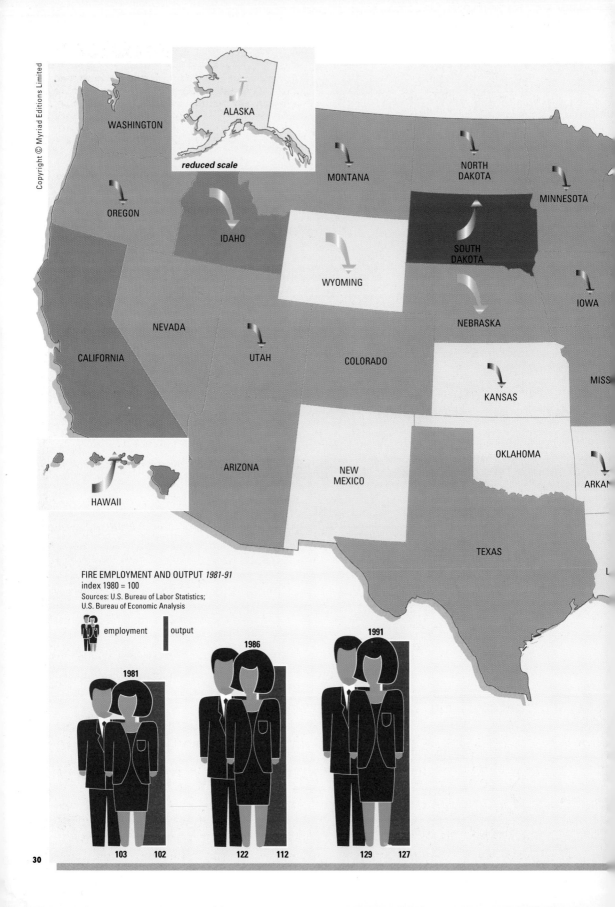

ALASKA

reduced scale

WASHINGTON

OREGON

MONTANA

NORTH
DAKOTA

MINNESOTA

IDAHO

SOUTH
DAKOTA

WYOMING

IOWA

NEVADA

NEBRASKA

CALIFORNIA

UTAH

COLORADO

MISS

KANSAS

HAWAII

ARIZONA

NEW
MEXICO

OKLAHOMA

ARKAN

TEXAS

L

FIRE EMPLOYMENT AND OUTPUT *1981-91*
index 1980 = 100

Sources: U.S. Bureau of Labor Statistics;
U.S. Bureau of Economic Analysis

employment | output

1981

103 102

1986

122 112

1991

129 127

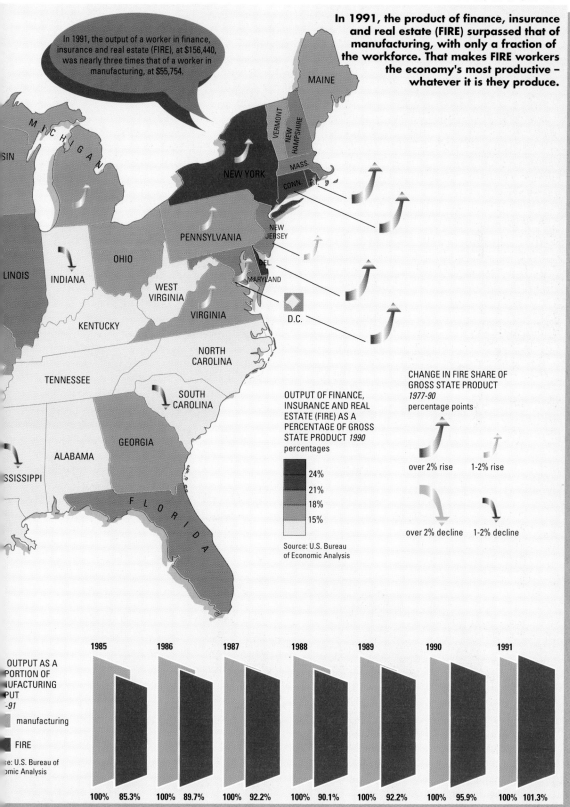

In 1991, the output of a worker in finance, insurance and real estate (FIRE), at $156,440, was nearly three times that of a worker in manufacturing, at $55,754.

In 1991, the product of finance, insurance and real estate (FIRE) surpassed that of manufacturing, with only a fraction of the workforce. That makes FIRE workers the economy's most productive – whatever it is they produce.

MICHIGAN

SIN

MAINE

VERMONT

NEW HAMPSHIRE

NEW YORK

MASS.

CONN. R.I.

ILLINOIS

INDIANA

OHIO

PENNSYLVANIA

NEW JERSEY

DEL.

MARYLAND

WEST VIRGINIA

VIRGINIA

D.C.

KENTUCKY

NORTH CAROLINA

TENNESSEE

SOUTH CAROLINA

GEORGIA

ALABAMA

SSISSIPPI

FLORIDA

OUTPUT OF FINANCE, INSURANCE AND REAL ESTATE (FIRE) AS A PERCENTAGE OF GROSS STATE PRODUCT *1990*
percentages

- 24%
- 21%
- 18%
- 15%

Source: U.S. Bureau of Economic Analysis

CHANGE IN FIRE SHARE OF GROSS STATE PRODUCT *1977-90*
percentage points

over 2% rise   1-2% rise

over 2% decline   1-2% decline

OUTPUT AS A PORTION OF MANUFACTURING OUTPUT -91

manufacturing

FIRE

Source: U.S. Bureau of Economic Analysis

1985	1986	1987	1988	1989	1990	1991
100% 85.3%	100% 89.7%	100% 92.2%	100% 90.1%	100% 92.2%	100% 95.9%	100% 101.3%

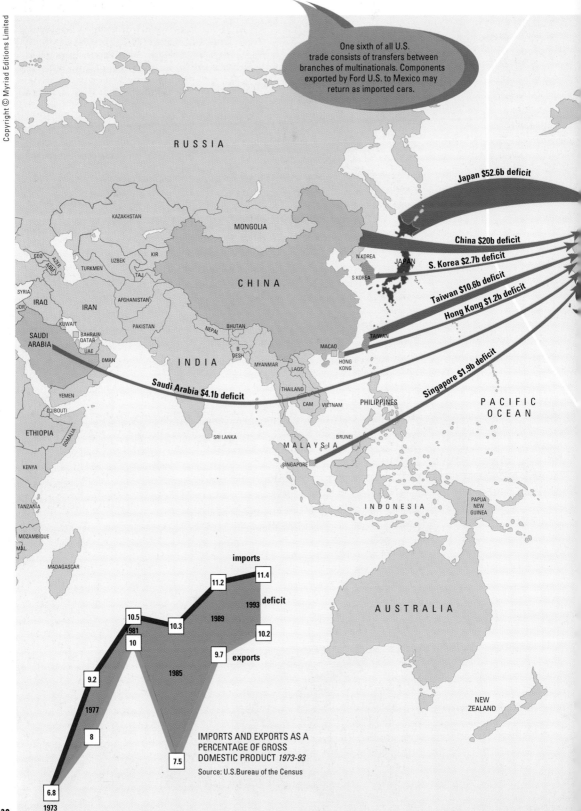

One sixth of all U.S. trade consists of transfers between branches of multinationals. Components exported by Ford U.S. to Mexico may return as imported cars.

Japan $52.6b deficit

China $20b deficit

S. Korea $2.7b deficit

Taiwan $10.6b deficit

Hong Kong $1.2b deficit

Saudi Arabia $4.1b deficit

Singapore $1.9b deficit

IMPORTS AND EXPORTS AS A PERCENTAGE OF GROSS DOMESTIC PRODUCT 1973-93
Source: U.S. Bureau of the Census

imports
deficit
exports

11.4
11.2
1993
1989
10.5
10.3
1981
10
10.2
9.7
1985
9.2
1977
8
7.5
6.8
1973

In 1992, before NAFTA, more than a quarter of all U.S. trade was with Canada and Mexico. The largest U.S. trade deficits were with Japan and China.

GREENLAND (Den)

CANADA

ICELAND

Germany $8.3b deficit

U.K. $2.2b surplus

Netherlands $8.2b surplus

Canada $10.8b deficit

UNITED STATES OF AMERICA

Belgium $5.2b surplus

France $0.6b deficit

Italy $4.1b deficit

Mexico $4.7b surplus

NORWAY · SWEDEN · FINLAND

RUSSIA

E LAT LITH

IRELAND · UNITED KINGDOM · DEN · BEL

NETH · BEL · GERMANY · POLAND · UKRAINE

FRANCE · CZ · S · AUS · HUNG · MOL · ROM

ITALY · S · B-H · YUG · BULG

PORTUGAL · SPAIN · ALB · M. · GREECE · TURKEY

BAHAMAS

CUBA · DOMINICAN REPUBLIC

In 1992, over half of all U.S. imports came from five countries: Canada (18%), Japan (18%), Mexico (7%), Germany and China (each 5%).

W SAHARA

MOROCCO

ALGERIA

LIBYA

EGYPT

TUNISIA

ISRAEL

MEXICO · BELIZE · HONDURAS · JAMAICA · HAITI · PUERTO RICO (US)

GUATEMALA
EL SALVADOR
NICARAGUA
COSTA RICA
PANAMA

TRINIDAD & TOBAGO

VENEZUELA · GUYANA · SURINAME · FRENCH GUIANA (Fr)

COLOMBIA

ECUADOR

PERU

BRAZIL

BOLIVIA

MAURITANIA

SENEGAL · GAMBIA

GUINEA-BISSAU · GUINEA

SIERRA LEONE · LIBERIA · IVORY COAST · GHANA · BENIN · TOGO · NIGERIA

MALI

NIGER

CHAD

SUDAN

BURKINA FASO

CAMEROON · EQ GUINEA · GABON · CONGO

CAR

ZAIRE

R. · B. · TANZ

UGANDA

ANGOLA

ZAMBIA

CHILE

ARGENTINA

EXPORTS BY STATE AS A PERCENTAGE OF TOTAL PERSONAL INCOME *1992*

ALAS.

WASH.

OREG.

IDAHO

MONT.

N.DAK.

S.DAK.

MINN.

WIS.

MICH.

ME.

VT. · N.H.

N.Y. · MASS. · CONN. · R.I.

NEV.

CALIF.

UTAH

WYO.

COLO.

NEBR.

IOWA

KANS.

MO.

ILL · IND.

OHIO

KY.

W.VA. · VA.

PA.

N.J.

MD. · DEL.

D.C.

ARIZ.

N.MEX.

OKLA.

ARK.

TENN.

N.C.

S.C.

GA.

MISS. · ALA.

HAWAII

TEX.

LA.

FLA.

BALANCE OF TRADE WITH TOP 15 TRADING PARTNERS
92 value in U.S. dollars

→ U.S. trade surplus

→ U.S. trade deficit

EXPORTS TO ITS TOP TRADING PARTNERS
a percentage of total exports *1992*

- over 5%
- 2.5-5%
- under 2.5%
- other countries

10%
8%
6%
4%

Source: U.S. Bureau of the Census

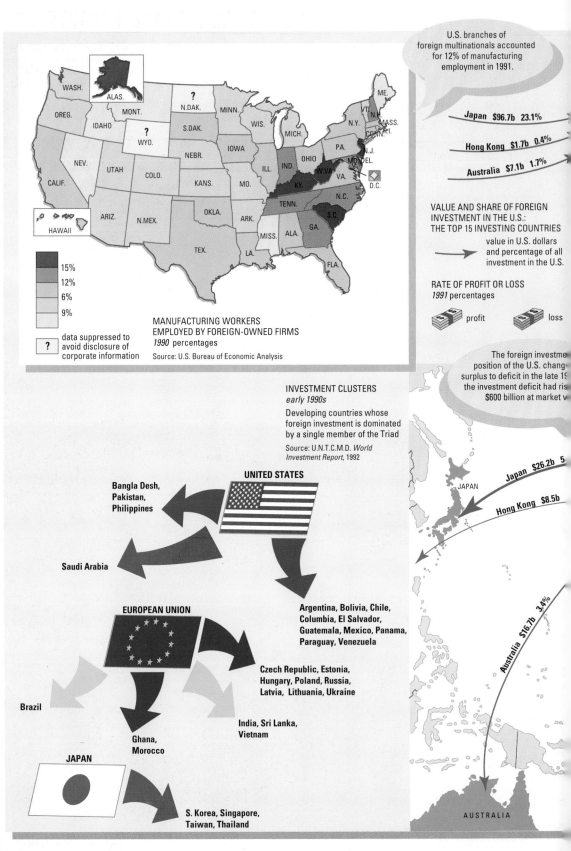

WASH. OREG. IDAHO MONT. N.DAK. ? MINN. WIS. MICH. ME. VT. N.H. MASS. N.Y. CONN. R.I. PA. N.J. DEL. MD. VA. W.VA. D.C. N.C. S.C. GA. FLA. ALA. MISS. LA. TEX. N.MEX. ARIZ. OKLA. ARK. TENN. KY. OHIO IND. ILL. MO. KANS. COLO. UTAH NEV. CALIF. WYO. ? S.DAK. NEBR. IOWA HAWAII ALAS.

15%
12%
6%
9%

? data suppressed to avoid disclosure of corporate information

MANUFACTURING WORKERS
EMPLOYED BY FOREIGN-OWNED FIRMS
1990 percentages
Source: U.S. Bureau of Economic Analysis

U.S. branches of
foreign multinationals accounted
for 12% of manufacturing
employment in 1991.

Japan **$96.7b 23.1%**

Hong Kong **$1.7b 0.4%**

Australia **$7.1b 1.7%**

VALUE AND SHARE OF FOREIGN
INVESTMENT IN THE U.S.:
THE TOP 15 INVESTING COUNTRIES

value in U.S. dollars
and percentage of all
investment in the U.S.

RATE OF PROFIT OR LOSS
1991 percentages

profit   loss

The foreign investme
position of the U.S. chang
surplus to deficit in the late 19
the investment deficit had ris
$600 billion at market v

INVESTMENT CLUSTERS
early 1990s

Developing countries whose
foreign investment is dominated
by a single member of the Triad

Source: U.N.T.C.M.D. *World
Investment Report*, 1992

UNITED STATES

**Bangla Desh,
Pakistan,
Philippines**

Saudi Arabia

EUROPEAN UNION

Brazil

JAPAN

**Argentina, Bolivia, Chile,
Columbia, El Salvador,
Guatemala, Mexico, Panama,
Paraguay, Venezuela**

**Czech Republic, Estonia,
Hungary, Poland, Russia,
Latvia, Lithuania, Ukraine**

**India, Sri Lanka,
Vietnam**

**Ghana,
Morocco**

**S. Korea, Singapore,
Taiwan, Thailand**

JAPAN

Japan **$26.2b 5**

Hong Kong **$8.5b**

Australia **$16.7b 3.4%**

AUSTRALIA

For long the world's leading investor,
the U.S. is now also a leading investee.
U.S. multinationals abroad are more profitable
than foreign-owned firms in the U.S.

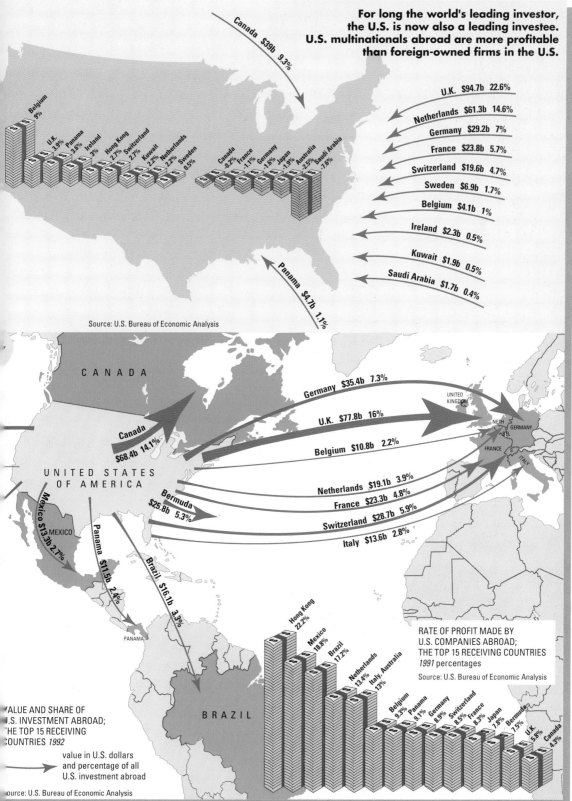

Canada $39b 9.3%

Belgium 9%
U.K. 3.3%
Panama 3.6%
Ireland 3%
Hong Kong 2.7%
Switzerland 2.7%
Kuwait 2.2%
Netherlands 2.2%
Sweden 0.5%

Canada -0.2%
France 1.1%
Germany -1.6%
Japan -1.9%
Australia 2.5%
Saudi Arabia 7.6%

U.K. $94.7b 22.6%
Netherlands $61.3b 14.6%
Germany $29.2b 7%
France $23.8b 5.7%
Switzerland $19.6b 4.7%
Sweden $6.9b 1.7%
Belgium $4.1b 1%
Ireland $2.3b 0.5%
Kuwait $1.9b 0.5%
Saudi Arabia $1.7b 0.4%

Panama $4.7b 1.1%

Source: U.S. Bureau of Economic Analysis

CANADA

UNITED STATES
OF AMERICA

Germany $35.4b 7.3%
U.K. $77.8b 16%
Belgium $10.8b 2.2%

Canada $68.4b 14.1%

Netherlands $19.1b 3.9%
France $23.3b 4.8%
Switzerland $28.7b 5.9%
Italy $13.6b 2.8%

Bermuda $25.8b 5.3%

Mexico $13.3b 2.7%
Panama $11.5b 2.4%
Brazil $16.1b 3.3%

MEXICO
PANAMA

UNITED KINGDOM
NETH
GERMANY
BEL
FRANCE
S
ITALY

BRAZIL

Hong Kong 22.2%
Mexico 18.8%
Brazil 17.2%
Netherlands 13.4%
Italy, Australia 13%
Belgium 9.3%
Panama 9.1%
Germany 8.9%
Switzerland 8.5%
France 8.3%
Japan 7.8%
Bermuda 7.5%
U.K. 5.8%
Canada 4.3%

RATE OF PROFIT MADE BY
U.S. COMPANIES ABROAD;
THE TOP 15 RECEIVING COUNTRIES
1991 percentages
Source: U.S. Bureau of Economic Analysis

VALUE AND SHARE OF
U.S. INVESTMENT ABROAD;
THE TOP 15 RECEIVING
COUNTRIES *1992*

value in U.S. dollars
and percentage of all
U.S. investment abroad

Source: U.S. Bureau of Economic Analysis

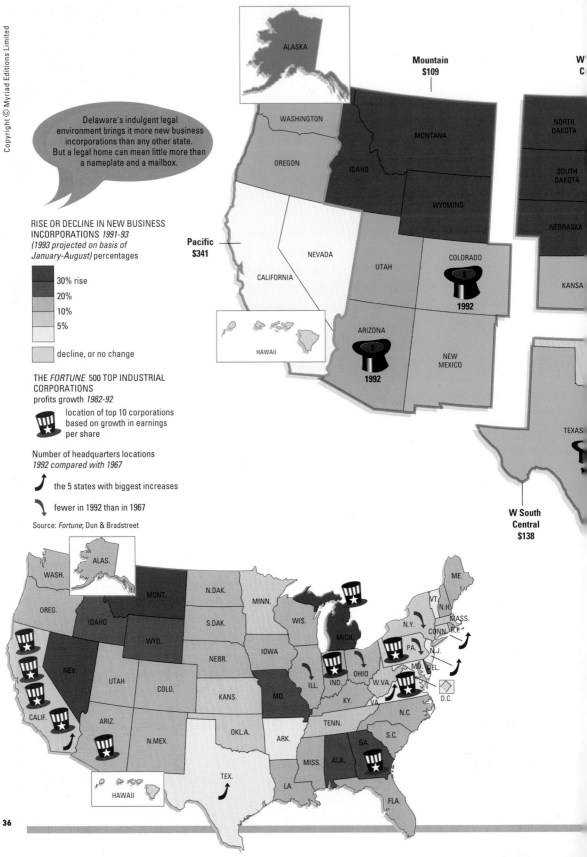

Delaware's indulgent legal
environment brings it more new business
incorporations than any other state.
But a legal home can mean little more than
a nameplate and a mailbox.

ALASKA

Mountain
$109

W
C

WASHINGTON

NORTH
DAKOTA

MONTANA

OREGON

SOUTH
DAKOTA

IDAHO

WYOMING

NEBRASKA

Pacific
$341

NEVADA

COLORADO

UTAH

CALIFORNIA

KANSA

1992

KANSA

**RISE OR DECLINE IN NEW BUSINESS
INCORPORATIONS** *1991-93*
*(1993 projected on basis of
January-August)* percentages

- 30% rise
- 20%
- 10%
- 5%
- decline, or no change

ARIZONA

NEW
MEXICO

1992

HAWAII

**THE *FORTUNE* 500 TOP INDUSTRIAL
CORPORATIONS**
profits growth *1982-92*

location of top 10 corporations
based on growth in earnings
per share

TEXAS

Number of headquarters locations
1992 compared with 1967

⤴ the 5 states with biggest increases

⤵ fewer in 1992 than in 1967

Source: *Fortune*; Dun & Bradstreet

W South
Central
$138

ALAS.

WASH.

ME.

MONT.

N.DAK.

MINN.

VT.
N.H.

OREG.

S.DAK.

WIS.

N.Y.

MASS.

IDAHO

MICH.

CONN. R.I.

WYO.

IOWA

PA.

N.J.

NEV.

NEBR.

OHIO

MD. DEL.

CALIF.

UTAH

COLO.

ILL.

IND.

W.VA.

D.C.

ARIZ.

KANS.

MO.

KY.

VA.

N.C.

N.MEX.

OKL.A.

ARK.

TENN.

S.C.

GA.

MISS.

ALA.

TEX.

LA.

FLA.

HAWAII

The boom years of the 1980s were followed by record-breaking insolvencies in the early 1990s. By 1993, the gloom began to lift and the pace of new business formation took off.

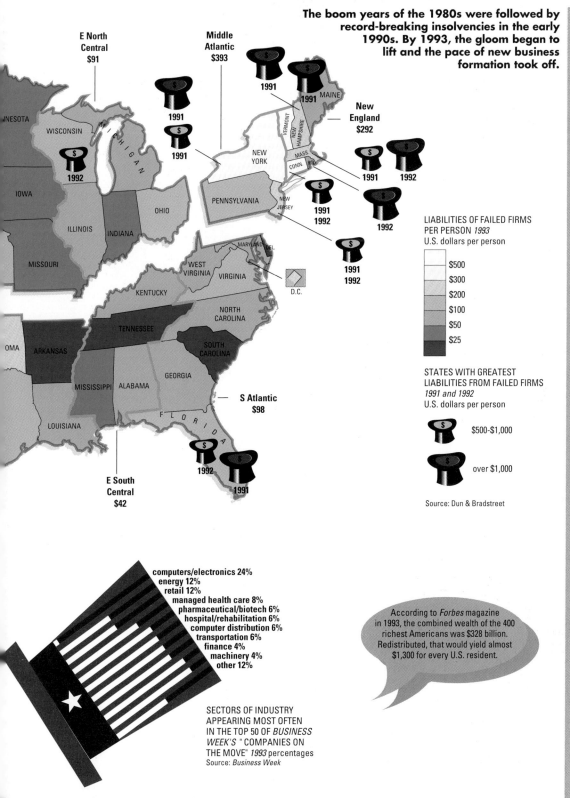

E North Central $91

Middle Atlantic $393

1991

1991

1991

MAINE

New England $292

1991

1992

1992

1992

1992

MINNESOTA

WISCONSIN

MICHIGAN

IOWA

ILLINOIS

INDIANA

OHIO

MISSOURI

NEW YORK

PENNSYLVANIA

VERMONT

NEW HAMPSHIRE

MASS.

CONN.

R.I.

NEW JERSEY

MARYLAND

DEL.

WEST VIRGINIA

VIRGINIA

D.C.

KENTUCKY

NORTH CAROLINA

TENNESSEE

OKLAHOMA

ARKANSAS

SOUTH CAROLINA

GEORGIA

MISSISSIPPI

ALABAMA

LOUISIANA

FLORIDA

S Atlantic $98

1992

1991

E South Central $42

1991

1992

LIABILITIES OF FAILED FIRMS PER PERSON *1993*
U.S. dollars per person

- $500
- $300
- $200
- $100
- $50
- $25

STATES WITH GREATEST LIABILITIES FROM FAILED FIRMS *1991 and 1992*
U.S. dollars per person

$500-$1,000

over $1,000

Source: Dun & Bradstreet

computers/electronics 24%
energy 12%
retail 12%
managed health care 8%
pharmaceutical/biotech 6%
hospital/rehabilitation 6%
computer distribution 6%
transportation 6%
finance 4%
machinery 4%
other 12%

SECTORS OF INDUSTRY APPEARING MOST OFTEN IN THE TOP 50 OF *BUSINESS WEEK'S* "COMPANIES ON THE MOVE" *1993* percentages
Source: *Business Week*

According to *Forbes* magazine in 1993, the combined wealth of the 400 richest Americans was $328 billion. Redistributed, that would yield almost $1,300 for every U.S. resident.

ALASKA

reduced scale

WASHINGTON

50

MONTANA

NORTH
DAKOTA

OREGON
3

IDAHO

SOUTH
DAKOTA

HAWAII
1

WYOMING

NEBRASKA

NEVADA
9

CALIFORNIA

UTAH

COLORADO
10

KANSA
43

95

OK

ARIZONA

NEW
MEXICO

29

TEXAS
48

U.S. 10

Canada 9

U.S. 864

U.K.,
W. Germany 5

Italy, France 4

Canada 632

Japan 3

Japan 394
U.K. 353
W. Germany 331
France 304
Italy 301

INTERNATIONAL COMPARISONS:
GREENHOUSE GAS EMISSIONS
AND MUNICIPAL WASTE
late 1980s or early 1990s

**greenhouse
gases**
*tonnes per
person per year*

**municipal
waste**
*kgs per
person per year*

1 kg = 2.2 lbs
1 tonne = 2,205 lbs

Source: *Human Development Report 1993*

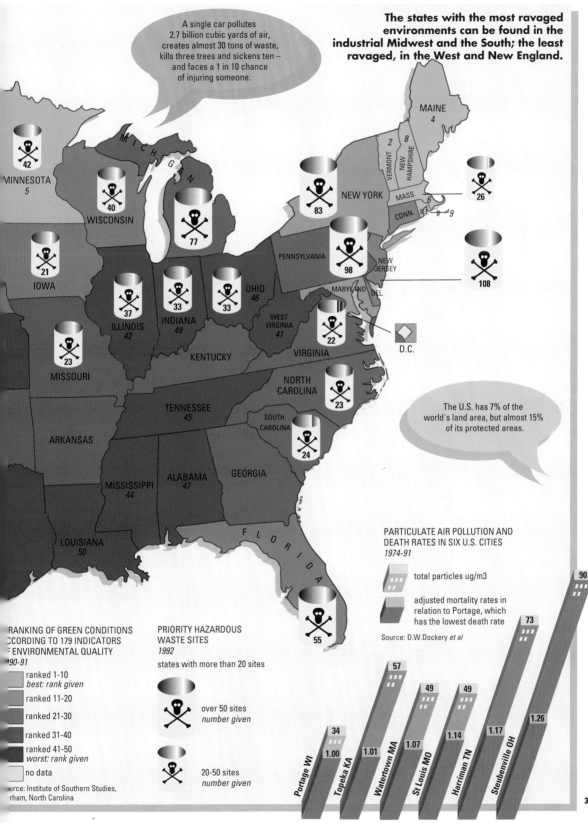

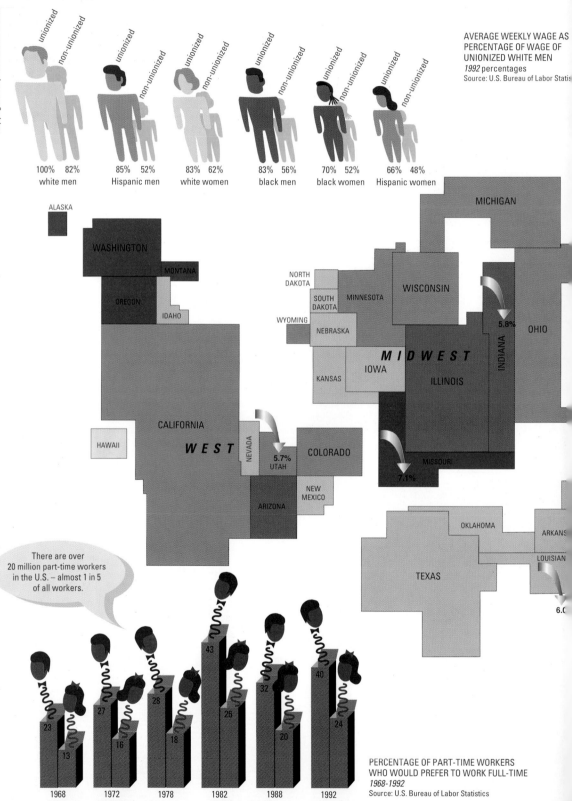

unionized   non-unionized

unionized   non-unionized

unionized   non-unionized

unionized   non-unionized

unionized   non-unionized

unionized   non-unionized

AVERAGE WEEKLY WAGE AS
PERCENTAGE OF WAGE OF
UNIONIZED WHITE MEN
1992 percentages
Source: U.S. Bureau of Labor Statis

100% 82%
white men

85% 52%
Hispanic men

83% 62%
white women

83% 56%
black men

70% 52%
black women

66% 48%
Hispanic women

ALASKA

MICHIGAN

WASHINGTON

MONTANA

OREGON

IDAHO

NORTH
DAKOTA

SOUTH
DAKOTA

MINNESOTA

WYOMING

NEBRASKA

WISCONSIN

5.8%

OHIO

INDIANA

M I D W E S T

IOWA

KANSAS

ILLINOIS

CALIFORNIA

W E S T

NEVADA

5.7%
UTAH

COLORADO

HAWAII

MISSOURI

7.1%

ARIZONA

NEW
MEXICO

OKLAHOMA

ARKANS

LOUISIAN

There are over
20 million part-time workers
in the U.S. – almost 1 in 5
of all workers.

TEXAS

6.0

43

28

27

32

40

23

26

24

16

18

20

13

1968   1972   1978   1982   1988   1992

PERCENTAGE OF PART-TIME WORKERS
WHO WOULD PREFER TO WORK FULL-TIME
1968-1992
Source: U.S. Bureau of Labor Statistics

Forty years ago, the unions represented almost a third of the U.S. labor force and wages were among the highest in the world. Now the U.S. is one of the least unionized countries of the rich world and wages are falling.

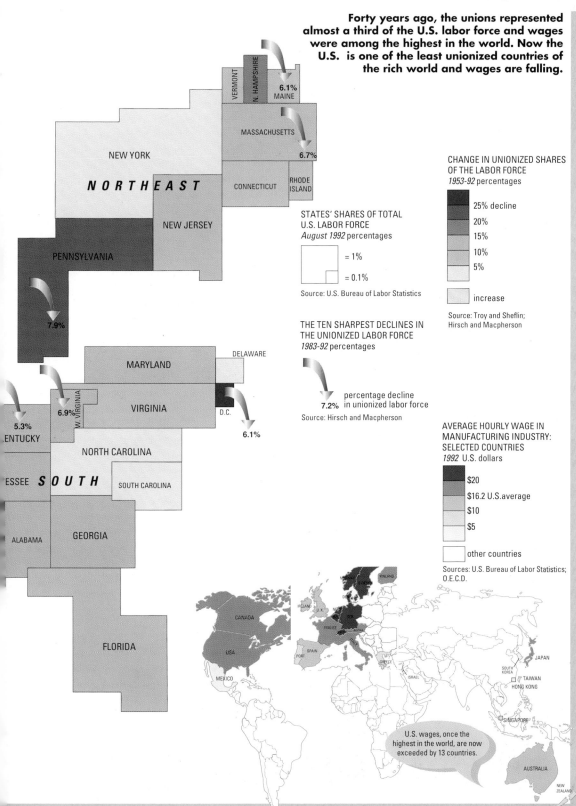

NORTHEAST

NEW YORK

VERMONT

N. HAMPSHIRE

6.1%
MAINE

MASSACHUSETTS

6.7%

CONNECTICUT

RHODE ISLAND

NEW JERSEY

PENNSYLVANIA

7.9%

MARYLAND

DELAWARE

W. VIRGINIA

VIRGINIA

D.C.

6.9%

6.1%

5.3%
KENTUCKY

NORTH CAROLINA

TENNESSEE **SOUTH**

SOUTH CAROLINA

ALABAMA

GEORGIA

FLORIDA

STATES' SHARES OF TOTAL U.S. LABOR FORCE
August 1992 percentages

☐ = 1%

▫ = 0.1%

Source: U.S. Bureau of Labor Statistics

THE TEN SHARPEST DECLINES IN THE UNIONIZED LABOR FORCE
1983-92 percentages

7.2% percentage decline in unionized labor force

Source: Hirsch and Macpherson

CHANGE IN UNIONIZED SHARES OF THE LABOR FORCE
1953-92 percentages

- 25% decline
- 20%
- 15%
- 10%
- 5%

☐ increase

Source: Troy and Sheflin; Hirsch and Macpherson

AVERAGE HOURLY WAGE IN MANUFACTURING INDUSTRY: SELECTED COUNTRIES
1992 U.S. dollars

- $20
- $16.2 U.S. average
- $10
- $5

☐ other countries

Sources: U.S. Bureau of Labor Statistics; O.E.C.D.

CANADA

USA

MEXICO

PORT

SPAIN

IRELAND

U.K.

FRANCE

GREECE

ISRAEL

FINLAND

SWEDEN

JAPAN

SOUTH KOREA

TAIWAN

HONG KONG

SINGAPORE

AUSTRALIA

NEW ZEALAND

U.S. wages, once the highest in the world, are now exceeded by 13 countries.

41

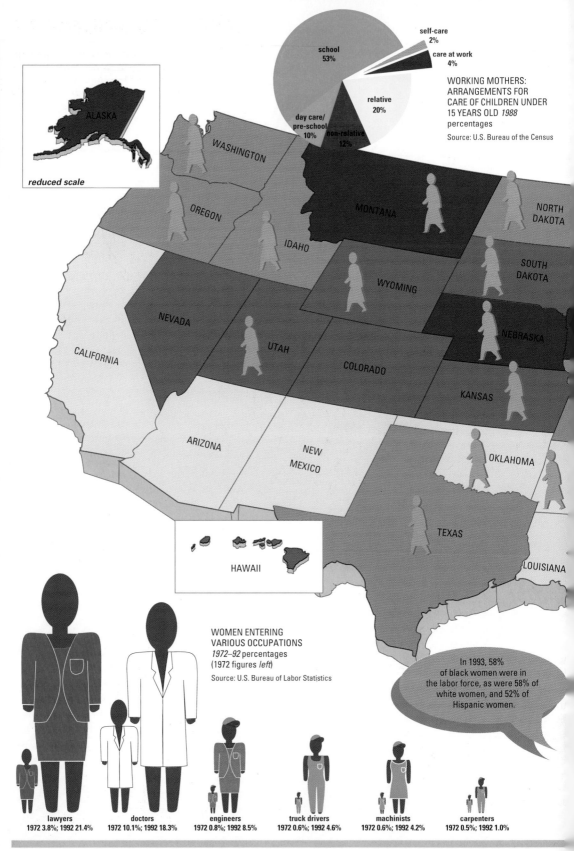

WORKING MOTHERS:
ARRANGEMENTS FOR
CARE OF CHILDREN UNDER
15 YEARS OLD *1988*
percentages
Source: U.S. Bureau of the Census

school
53%

self-care
2%

care at work
4%

relative
20%

non-relative
12%

day care/
pre-school
10%

ALASKA
reduced scale

WASHINGTON

OREGON

IDAHO

MONTANA

NORTH
DAKOTA

WYOMING

SOUTH
DAKOTA

NEVADA

UTAH

COLORADO

NEBRASKA

CALIFORNIA

KANSAS

ARIZONA

NEW
MEXICO

OKLAHOMA

TEXAS

LOUISIANA

HAWAII

WOMEN ENTERING
VARIOUS OCCUPATIONS
1972–92 percentages
(1972 figures *left*)
Source: U.S. Bureau of Labor Statistics

In 1993, 58%
of black women were in
the labor force, as were 58% of
white women, and 52% of
Hispanic women.

lawyers
1972 3.8%; 1992 21.4%

doctors
1972 10.1%; 1992 18.3%

engineers
1972 0.8%; 1992 8.5%

truck drivers
1972 0.6%; 1992 4.6%

machinists
1972 0.6%; 1992 4.2%

carpenters
1972 0.5%; 1992 1.0%

In the early 1990s nearly 60 percent of all women were in the labor force, almost double the share in 1950.

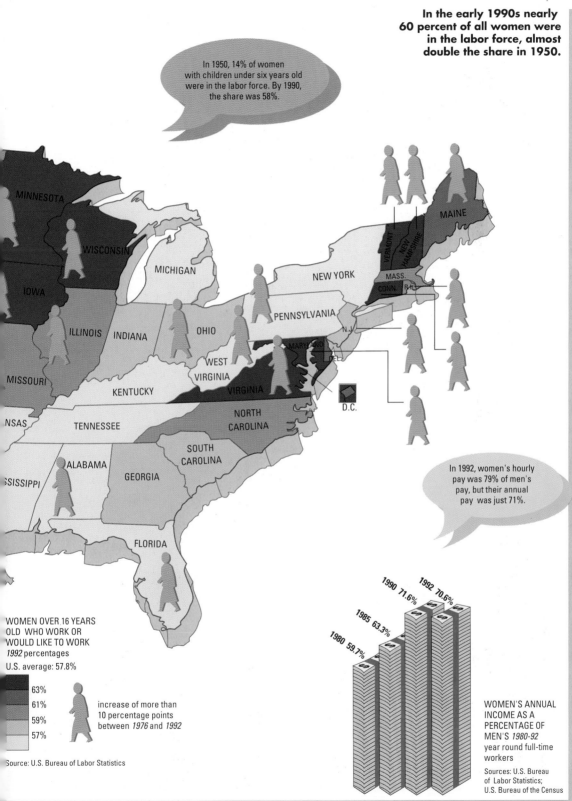

In 1950, 14% of women with children under six years old were in the labor force. By 1990, the share was 58%.

In 1992, women's hourly pay was 79% of men's pay, but their annual pay was just 71%.

MINNESOTA

WISCONSIN

IOWA

MICHIGAN

NEW YORK

MAINE

VERMONT

NEW HAMPSHIRE

MASS.

CONN. R.I.

ILLINOIS INDIANA OHIO

PENNSYLVANIA

N.J.

MISSOURI

WEST VIRGINIA

MARYLAND

DEL.

KENTUCKY

VIRGINIA

D.C.

NSAS

TENNESSEE

NORTH CAROLINA

ALABAMA GEORGIA

SOUTH CAROLINA

SSISSIPPI

FLORIDA

WOMEN OVER 16 YEARS OLD WHO WORK OR WOULD LIKE TO WORK
1992 percentages
U.S. average: 57.8%

- 63%
- 61%
- 59%
- 57%

increase of more than 10 percentage points between *1976* and *1992*

Source: U.S. Bureau of Labor Statistics

1980 59.7%
1985 63.3%
1990 71.6%
1992 70.6%

WOMEN'S ANNUAL INCOME AS A PERCENTAGE OF MEN'S *1980-92* year round full-time workers

Sources: U.S. Bureau of Labor Statistics; U.S. Bureau of the Census

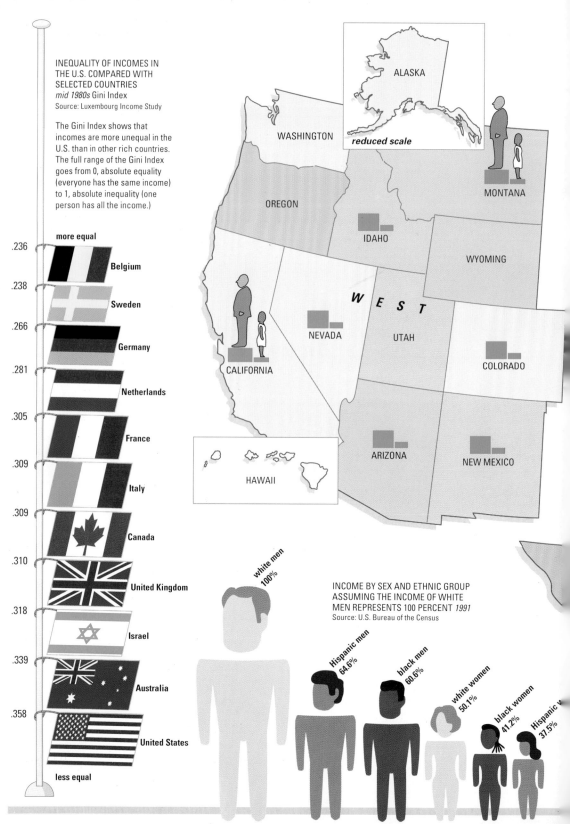

Copyright © Myriad Editions Limited

INEQUALITY OF INCOMES IN
THE U.S. COMPARED WITH
SELECTED COUNTRIES
mid 1980s Gini Index
Source: Luxembourg Income Study

The Gini Index shows that
incomes are more unequal in the
U.S. than in other rich countries.
The full range of the Gini Index
goes from 0, absolute equality
(everyone has the same income)
to 1, absolute inequality (one
person has all the income.)

more equal

.236 — Belgium

.238 — Sweden

.266 — Germany

.281 — Netherlands

.305 — France

.309 — Italy

.309 — Canada

.310 — United Kingdom

.318 — Israel

.339 — Australia

.358 — United States

less equal

ALASKA

reduced scale

WASHINGTON

OREGON

IDAHO

MONTANA

WYOMING

W E S T

NEVADA

UTAH

CALIFORNIA

COLORADO

ARIZONA

NEW MEXICO

HAWAII

INCOME BY SEX AND ETHNIC GROUP
ASSUMING THE INCOME OF WHITE
MEN REPRESENTS 100 PERCENT *1991*
Source: U.S. Bureau of the Census

white men 100%

Hispanic men 64.6%

black men 60.6%

white women 50.1%

black women 41.2%

Hispanic women 37.5%

44

Incomes are often most unequal in affluent states housing the super rich.

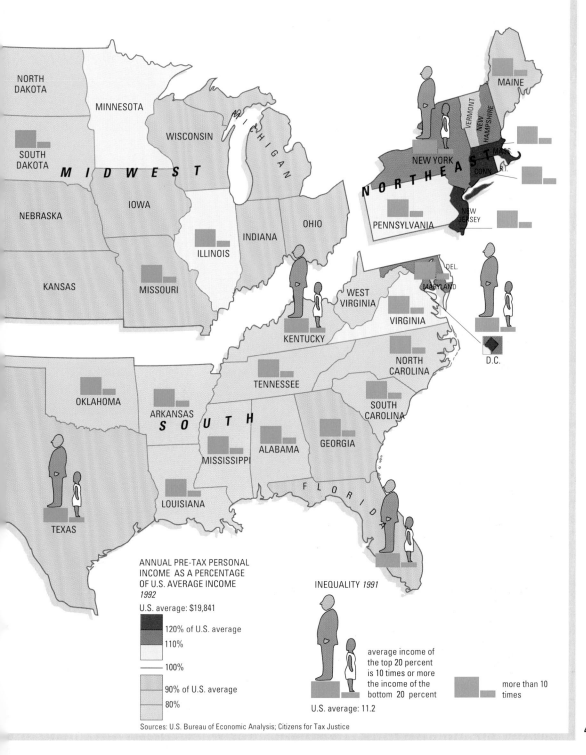

ANNUAL PRE-TAX PERSONAL
INCOME AS A PERCENTAGE
OF U.S. AVERAGE INCOME
1992

U.S. average: $19,841

- 120% of U.S. average
- 110%
- 100%
- 90% of U.S. average
- 80%

INEQUALITY *1991*

average income of
the top 20 percent
is 10 times or more
the income of the
bottom 20 percent

more than 10
times

U.S. average: 11.2

Sources: U.S. Bureau of Economic Analysis; Citizens for Tax Justice

45

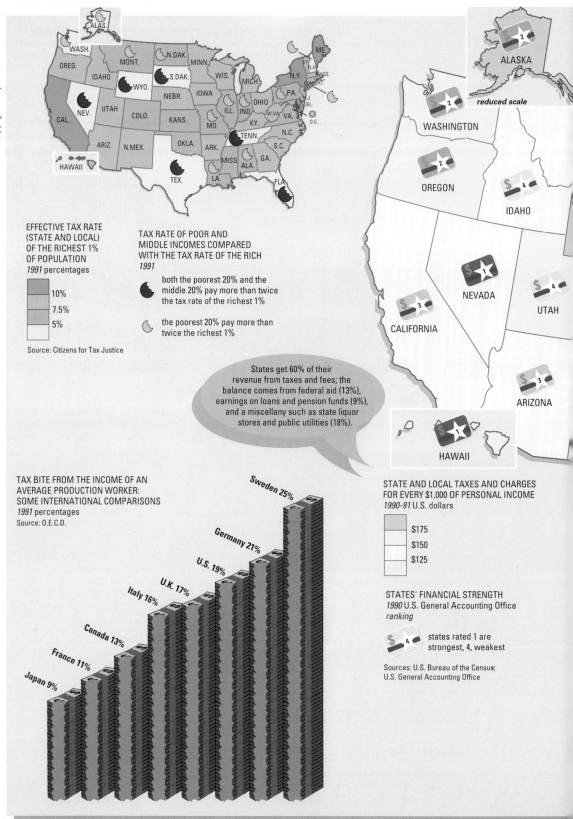

EFFECTIVE TAX RATE (STATE AND LOCAL) OF THE RICHEST 1% OF POPULATION
1991 percentages

- 10%
- 7.5%
- 5%

Source: Citizens for Tax Justice

TAX RATE OF POOR AND MIDDLE INCOMES COMPARED WITH THE TAX RATE OF THE RICH
1991

🌑 both the poorest 20% and the middle 20% pay more than twice the tax rate of the richest 1%

🌒 the poorest 20% pay more than twice the richest 1%

States get 60% of their revenue from taxes and fees; the balance comes from federal aid (13%), earnings on loans and pension funds (9%), and a miscellany such as state liquor stores and public utilities (18%).

TAX BITE FROM THE INCOME OF AN AVERAGE PRODUCTION WORKER: SOME INTERNATIONAL COMPARISONS
1991 percentages
Source: O.E.C.D.

Sweden 25%
Germany 21%
U.S. 19%
U.K. 17%
Italy 16%
Canada 13%
France 11%
Japan 9%

STATE AND LOCAL TAXES AND CHARGES FOR EVERY $1,000 OF PERSONAL INCOME
1990-91 U.S. dollars

- $175
- $150
- $125

STATES' FINANCIAL STRENGTH
1990 U.S. General Accounting Office *ranking*

states rated 1 are strongest, 4, weakest

Sources: U.S. Bureau of the Census; U.S. General Accounting Office

ALASKA   reduced scale
WASHINGTON
OREGON
IDAHO
NEVADA
UTAH
CALIFORNIA
ARIZONA
HAWAII

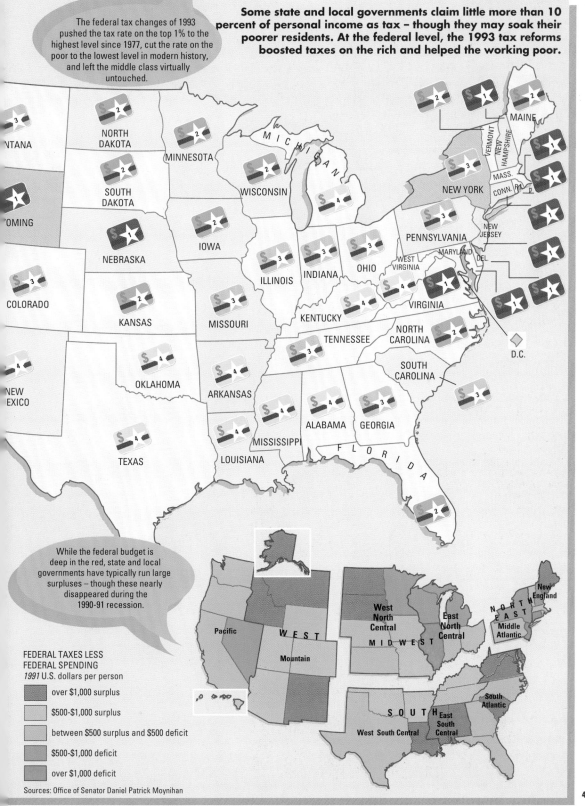

Some state and local governments claim little more than 10 percent of personal income as tax – though they may soak their poorer residents. At the federal level, the 1993 tax reforms boosted taxes on the rich and helped the working poor.

The federal tax changes of 1993 pushed the tax rate on the top 1% to the highest level since 1977, cut the rate on the poor to the lowest level in modern history, and left the middle class virtually untouched.

While the federal budget is deep in the red, state and local governments have typically run large surpluses – though these nearly disappeared during the 1990-91 recession.

FEDERAL TAXES LESS FEDERAL SPENDING
1991 U.S. dollars per person

- over $1,000 surplus
- $500-$1,000 surplus
- between $500 surplus and $500 deficit
- $500-$1,000 deficit
- over $1,000 deficit

Sources: Office of Senator Daniel Patrick Moynihan

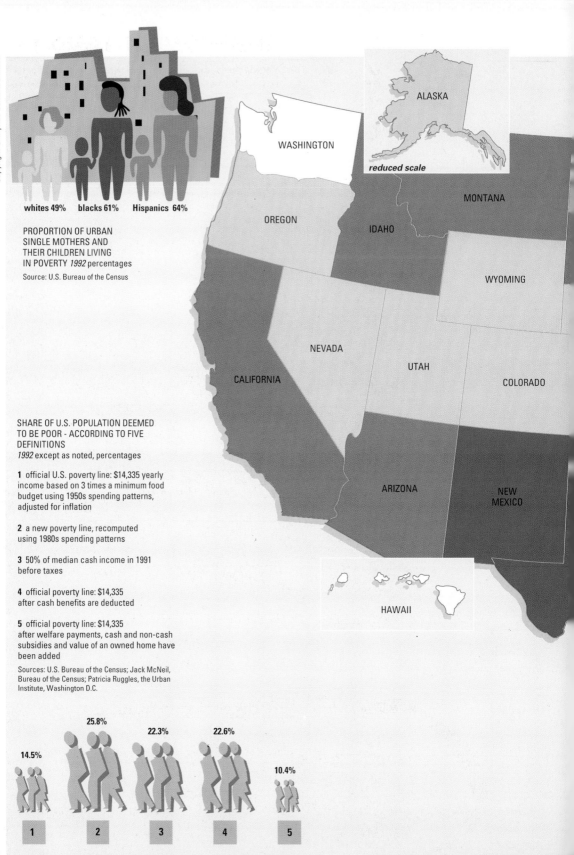

whites 49%   blacks 61%   Hispanics 64%

PROPORTION OF URBAN
SINGLE MOTHERS AND
THEIR CHILDREN LIVING
IN POVERTY *1992* percentages

Source: U.S. Bureau of the Census

SHARE OF U.S. POPULATION DEEMED
TO BE POOR - ACCORDING TO FIVE
DEFINITIONS
1992 except as noted, percentages

1 official U.S. poverty line: $14,335 yearly
income based on 3 times a minimum food
budget using 1950s spending patterns,
adjusted for inflation

2 a new poverty line, recomputed
using 1980s spending patterns

3 50% of median cash income in 1991
before taxes

4 official poverty line: $14,335
after cash benefits are deducted

5 official poverty line: $14,335
after welfare payments, cash and non-cash
subsidies and value of an owned home have
been added

Sources: U.S. Bureau of the Census; Jack McNeil,
Bureau of the Census; Patricia Ruggles, the Urban
Institute, Washington D.C.

14.5%   25.8%   22.3%   22.6%   10.4%

1   2   3   4   5

WASHINGTON

OREGON

ALASKA

reduced scale

MONTANA

IDAHO

WYOMING

NEVADA

UTAH

COLORADO

CALIFORNIA

ARIZONA

NEW
MEXICO

HAWAII

THE PROMISED LAND 18

The U.S. has more poor and near-poor than any other rich country – and the smallest middle class.

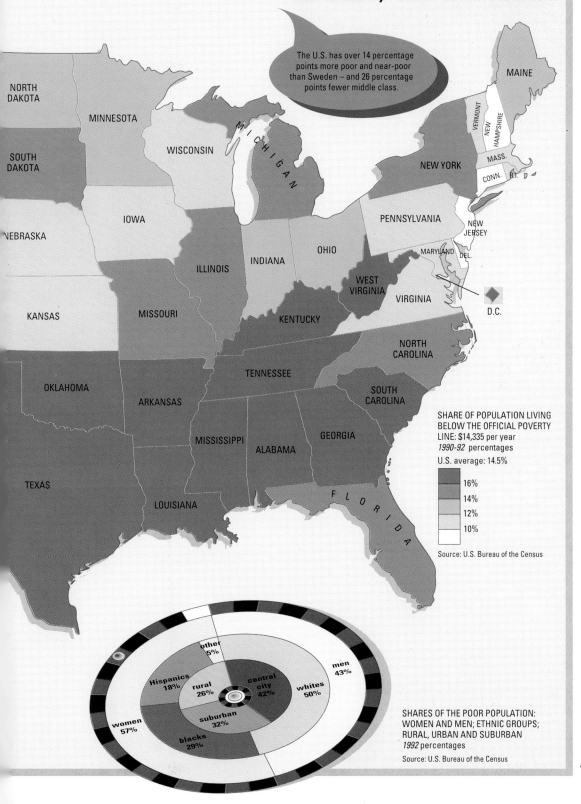

The U.S. has over 14 percentage points more poor and near-poor than Sweden – and 26 percentage points fewer middle class.

NORTH DAKOTA
MINNESOTA
SOUTH DAKOTA
WISCONSIN
MICHIGAN
MAINE
VERMONT
NEW HAMPSHIRE
NEW YORK
MASS.
CONN.
R.I.
IOWA
NEBRASKA
PENNSYLVANIA
NEW JERSEY
OHIO
INDIANA
ILLINOIS
MARYLAND
DEL.
KANSAS
MISSOURI
WEST VIRGINIA
VIRGINIA
D.C.
KENTUCKY
NORTH CAROLINA
TENNESSEE
OKLAHOMA
ARKANSAS
SOUTH CAROLINA
MISSISSIPPI
ALABAMA
GEORGIA
TEXAS
LOUISIANA
FLORIDA

SHARE OF POPULATION LIVING BELOW THE OFFICIAL POVERTY LINE: $14,335 per year
1990-92 percentages
U.S. average: 14.5%

- 16%
- 14%
- 12%
- 10%

Source: U.S. Bureau of the Census

other 5%
Hispanics 18%
rural 26%
central city 42%
whites 50%
men 43%
women 57%
suburban 32%
blacks 29%

SHARES OF THE POOR POPULATION: WOMEN AND MEN; ETHNIC GROUPS; RURAL, URBAN AND SUBURBAN
1992 percentages
Source: U.S. Bureau of the Census

49

.83
Poland

.86
Russia

.87
U.S. Hispanic

.88
U.S. black

.92
Italy
Ireland

.95
Germany

.96
U.K.

.97
France
Netherlands
Sweden
Norway
U.S. all

.98
U.S. white

A selected development index showing the largest
U.S. ethnic groups, and countries reflecting the
ancestry of Americans (as declared in the 1990
Census)
*based on income, literacy rates, average
years of schooling, and life expectancy 1993*

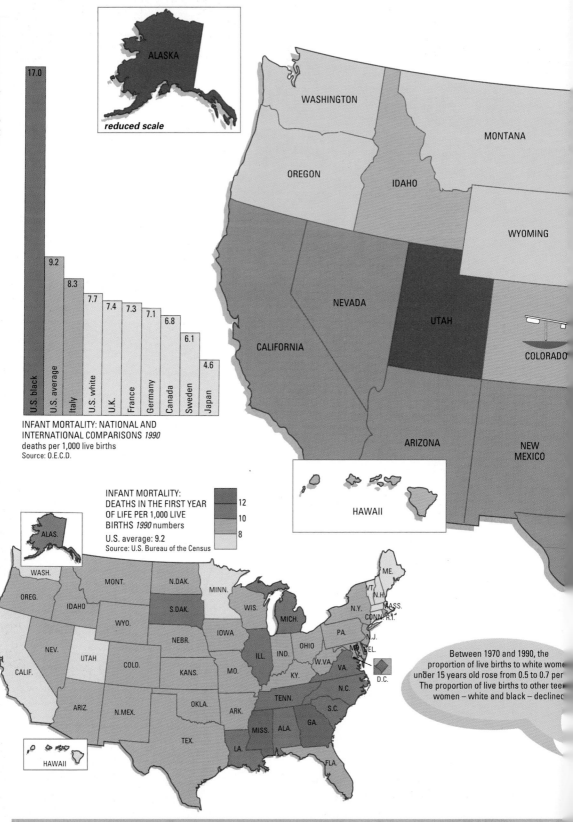

ALASKA
reduced scale

17.0
9.2
8.3
7.7
7.4
7.3
7.1
6.8
6.1
4.6

U.S. black
U.S. average
Italy
U.S. white
U.K.
France
Germany
Canada
Sweden
Japan

INFANT MORTALITY: NATIONAL AND
INTERNATIONAL COMPARISONS *1990*
deaths per 1,000 live births
Source: O.E.C.D.

WASHINGTON
MONTANA
OREGON
IDAHO
WYOMING
NEVADA
UTAH
COLORADO
CALIFORNIA
ARIZONA
NEW MEXICO

INFANT MORTALITY:
DEATHS IN THE FIRST YEAR
OF LIFE PER 1,000 LIVE
BIRTHS *1990* numbers

U.S. average: 9.2
Source: U.S. Bureau of the Census

12
10
8

HAWAII

ALAS.

WASH.
OREG.
IDAHO
MONT.
N.DAK.
MINN.
WIS.
S.DAK.
WYO.
NEBR.
IOWA
MICH.
N.Y.
ME.
VT.
N.H.
MASS.
CONN. R.I.
PA.
N.J.
NEV.
UTAH
COLO.
KANS.
MO.
ILL.
IND.
OHIO
W.VA.
VA.
MD.
DEL.
D.C.
CALIF.
ARIZ.
N.MEX.
OKLA.
ARK.
KY.
TENN.
N.C.
S.C.
MISS.
ALA.
GA.
TEX.
LA.
FLA.

HAWAII

Between 1970 and 1990, the
proportion of live births to white wome[n]
under 15 years old rose from 0.5 to 0.7 per
The proportion of live births to other tee[n]
women – white and black – decline[d]

The Southwest has more newborns than any other region, while the South has the highest share of infant mortality and babies born with seriously low weight.

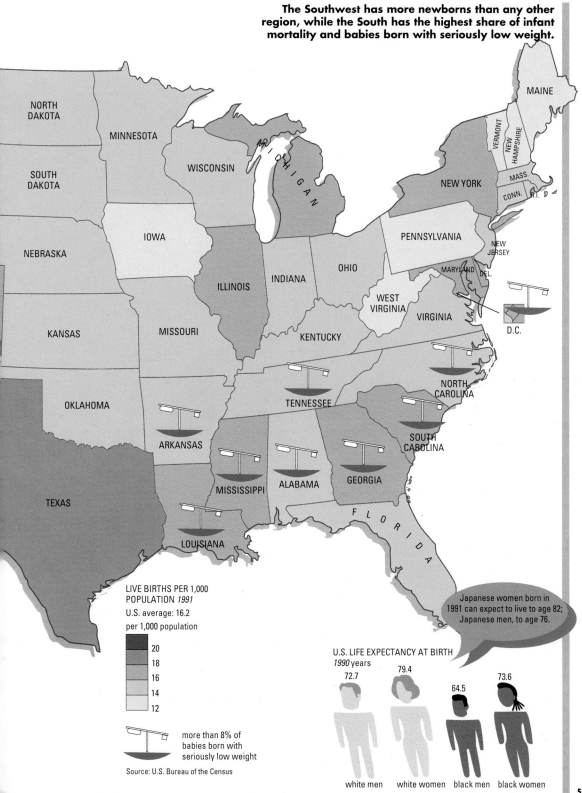

NORTH DAKOTA

MINNESOTA

MAINE

SOUTH DAKOTA

WISCONSIN

MICHIGAN

VERMONT

NEW HAMPSHIRE

NEW YORK

MASS.

CONN.

R.I.

NEBRASKA

IOWA

PENNSYLVANIA

NEW JERSEY

ILLINOIS

INDIANA

OHIO

MARYLAND

DEL.

KANSAS

MISSOURI

WEST VIRGINIA

VIRGINIA

D.C.

KENTUCKY

OKLAHOMA

TENNESSEE

NORTH CAROLINA

ARKANSAS

SOUTH CAROLINA

TEXAS

MISSISSIPPI

ALABAMA

GEORGIA

LOUISIANA

FLORIDA

LIVE BIRTHS PER 1,000 POPULATION *1991*

U.S. average: 16.2 per 1,000 population

- 20
- 18
- 16
- 14
- 12

more than 8% of babies born with seriously low weight

Source: U.S. Bureau of the Census

Japanese women born in 1991 can expect to live to age 82; Japanese men, to age 76.

U.S. LIFE EXPECTANCY AT BIRTH
1990 years

72.7 79.4 64.5 73.6

white men   white women   black men   black women

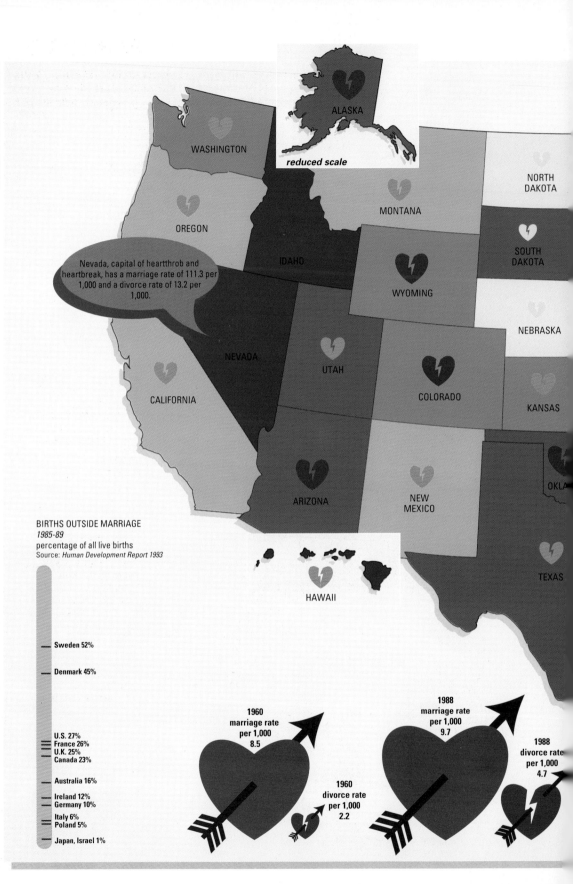

ALASKA
reduced scale

WASHINGTON

OREGON

MONTANA

IDAHO

NORTH DAKOTA

SOUTH DAKOTA

WYOMING

NEBRASKA

Nevada, capital of heartthrob and heartbreak, has a marriage rate of 111.3 per 1,000 and a divorce rate of 13.2 per 1,000.

NEVADA

UTAH

COLORADO

KANSAS

CALIFORNIA

ARIZONA

NEW MEXICO

OKLA

TEXAS

HAWAII

BIRTHS OUTSIDE MARRIAGE
1985-89
percentage of all live births
Source: *Human Development Report 1993*

Sweden 52%

Denmark 45%

U.S. 27%
France 26%
U.K. 25%
Canada 23%

Australia 16%

Ireland 12%
Germany 10%

Italy 6%
Poland 5%

Japan, Israel 1%

1960 marriage rate per 1,000 8.5

1960 divorce rate per 1,000 2.2

1988 marriage rate per 1,000 9.7

1988 divorce rate per 1,000 4.7

The rate of marriage has changed little since the 1960s, while the rate of divorce has doubled. Many more people now live alone or as single-parent families.

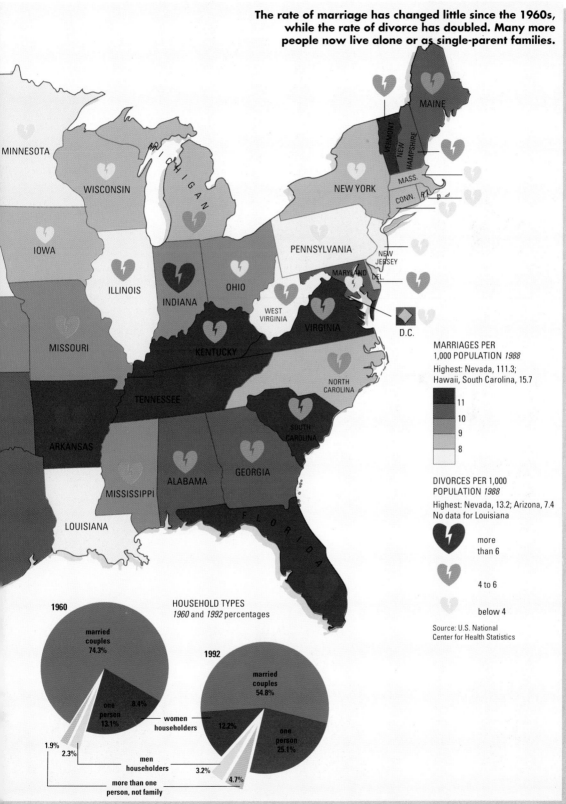

MINNESOTA

WISCONSIN

MICHIGAN

IOWA

ILLINOIS

INDIANA

OHIO

PENNSYLVANIA

NEW YORK

MAINE

VERMONT

NEW HAMPSHIRE

MASS.

CONN. R.I.

NEW JERSEY

MARYLAND

DEL.

D.C.

MISSOURI

KENTUCKY

WEST VIRGINIA

VIRGINIA

NORTH CAROLINA

TENNESSEE

ARKANSAS

SOUTH CAROLINA

MISSISSIPPI

ALABAMA

GEORGIA

LOUISIANA

FLORIDA

MARRIAGES PER 1,000 POPULATION *1988*

Highest: Nevada, 111.3; Hawaii, South Carolina, 15.7

- 11
- 10
- 9
- 8

DIVORCES PER 1,000 POPULATION *1988*

Highest: Nevada, 13.2; Arizona, 7.4
No data for Louisiana

more than 6

4 to 6

below 4

Source: U.S. National Center for Health Statistics

HOUSEHOLD TYPES
1960 and *1992* percentages

1960

married couples 74.3%

one person 13.1%

8.4% women householders

1.9%

2.3% men householders

more than one person, not family

1992

married couples 54.8%

one person 25.1%

12.2%

3.2%

4.7%

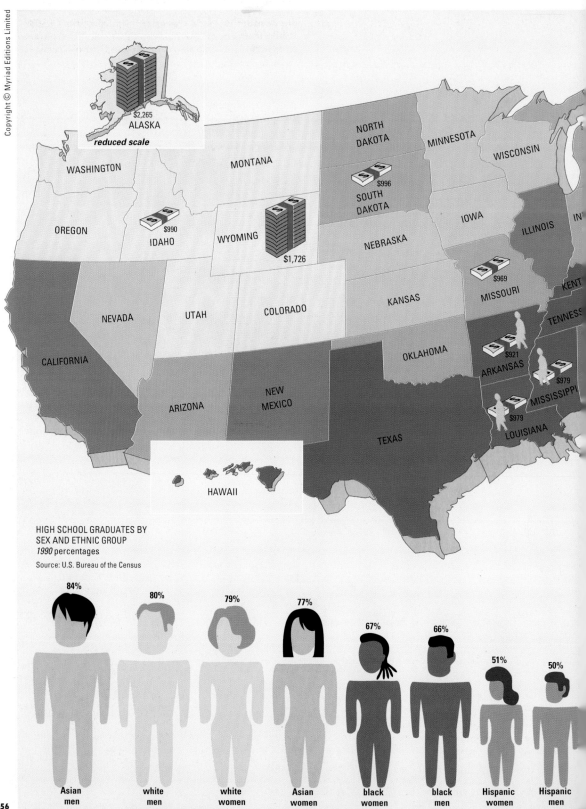

$2,265
ALASKA
reduced scale

WASHINGTON

MONTANA

NORTH DAKOTA

MINNESOTA

WISCONSIN

OREGON

$990
IDAHO

WYOMING

$1,726

$996
SOUTH DAKOTA

NEBRASKA

IOWA

ILLINOIS

IN

$969
MISSOURI

KENT

NEVADA

UTAH

COLORADO

KANSAS

TENNESS

CALIFORNIA

OKLAHOMA

$921
ARKANSAS

$979

ARIZONA

NEW MEXICO

$979
LOUISIANA

MISSISSIPPI

TEXAS

HAWAII

HIGH SCHOOL GRADUATES BY SEX AND ETHNIC GROUP
1990 percentages

Source: U.S. Bureau of the Census

84%	80%	79%	77%	67%	66%	51%	50%
Asian men	white men	white women	Asian women	black women	black men	Hispanic women	Hispanic men

Despite higher levels of formal education, in the early 1990s only one in five Americans reached a high standard of literacy.

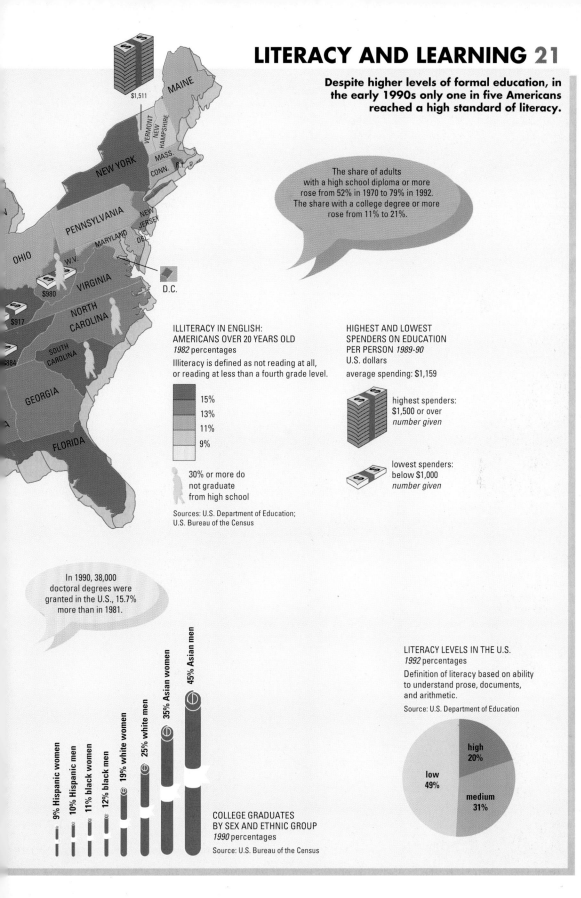

$1,511

MAINE

VERMONT
NEW HAMPSHIRE
MASS.
CONN. R.I.

NEW YORK

PENNSYLVANIA

NEW JERSEY

MARYLAND
DEL.

OHIO

W.V.

$980

VIRGINIA

D.C.

NORTH CAROLINA

$917

SOUTH CAROLINA

$884

GEORGIA

FLORIDA

The share of adults with a high school diploma or more rose from 52% in 1970 to 79% in 1992. The share with a college degree or more rose from 11% to 21%.

ILLITERACY IN ENGLISH: AMERICANS OVER 20 YEARS OLD
1982 percentages

Illiteracy is defined as not reading at all, or reading at less than a fourth grade level.

- 15%
- 13%
- 11%
- 9%

30% or more do not graduate from high school

Sources: U.S. Department of Education; U.S. Bureau of the Census

HIGHEST AND LOWEST SPENDERS ON EDUCATION PER PERSON *1989-90*
U.S. dollars

average spending: $1,159

highest spenders: $1,500 or over *number given*

lowest spenders: below $1,000 *number given*

In 1990, 38,000 doctoral degrees were granted in the U.S., 15.7% more than in 1981.

9% Hispanic women

10% Hispanic men

11% black women

12% black men

19% white women

25% white men

35% Asian women

45% Asian men

COLLEGE GRADUATES BY SEX AND ETHNIC GROUP
1990 percentages

Source: U.S. Bureau of the Census

LITERACY LEVELS IN THE U.S.
1992 percentages

Definition of literacy based on ability to understand prose, documents, and arithmetic.

Source: U.S. Department of Education

high 20%

medium 31%

low 49%

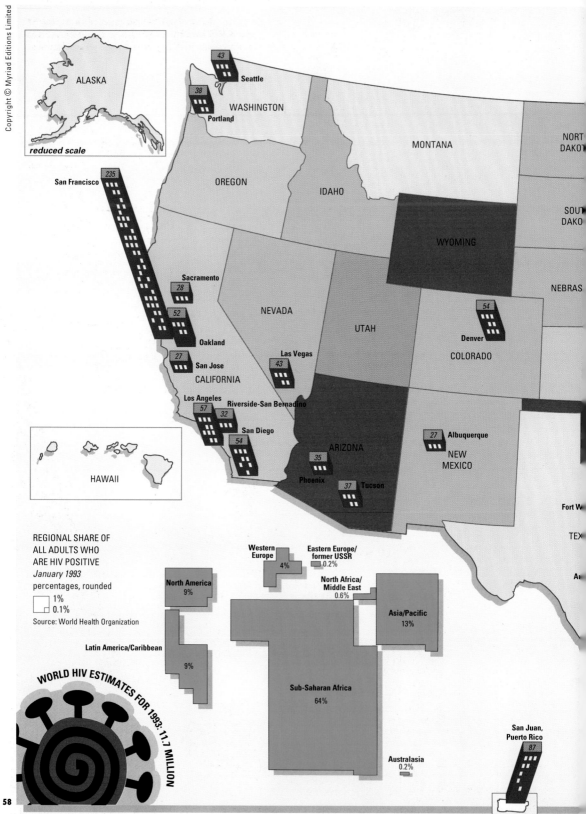

ALASKA

reduced scale

43

Seattle

WASHINGTON

38

Portland

MONTANA

NORT
DAKOT

OREGON

IDAHO

235

San Francisco

SOU
DAKO

Sacramento

28

52

Oakland

NEVADA

UTAH

WYOMING

NEBRAS

54

Denver

COLORADO

27

San Jose

CALIFORNIA

Las Vegas

43

Los Angeles

57 32 Riverside-San Bernadino

San Diego

54

ARIZONA

27 Albuquerque

NEW
MEXICO

HAWAII

35

Phoenix

37 Tucson

Fort W

TEX

A

REGIONAL SHARE OF
ALL ADULTS WHO
ARE HIV POSITIVE
January 1993
percentages, rounded

☐ 1%
☐ 0.1%

Source: World Health Organization

Western
Europe

4%

Eastern Europe/
former USSR
0.2%

North America
9%

North Africa/
Middle East
0.6%

Asia/Pacific
13%

Latin America/Caribbean

9%

Sub-Saharan Africa
64%

WORLD HIV ESTIMATES FOR 1993: 11.7 MILLION

San Juan,
Puerto Rico

87

Australasia
0.2%

More than 80 percent of Americans with AIDS live in large cities – but the rate of increase in AIDS is higher in many rural states.

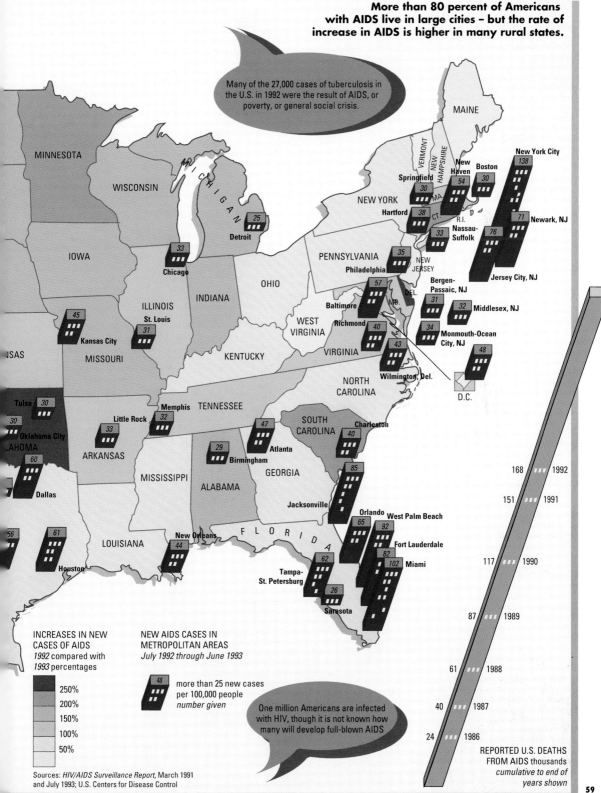

Many of the 27,000 cases of tuberculosis in the U.S. in 1992 were the result of AIDS, or poverty, or general social crisis.

One million Americans are infected with HIV, though it is not known how many will develop full-blown AIDS

INCREASES IN NEW CASES OF AIDS
1992 compared with *1993* percentages

- 250%
- 200%
- 150%
- 100%
- 50%

NEW AIDS CASES IN METROPOLITAN AREAS
July 1992 through June 1993

48 — more than 25 new cases per 100,000 people *number given*

REPORTED U.S. DEATHS FROM AIDS thousands *cumulative to end of years shown*

168	1992
151	1991
117	1990
87	1989
61	1988
40	1987
24	1986

Sources: *HIV/AIDS Surveillance Report*, March 1991 and July 1993; U.S. Centers for Disease Control

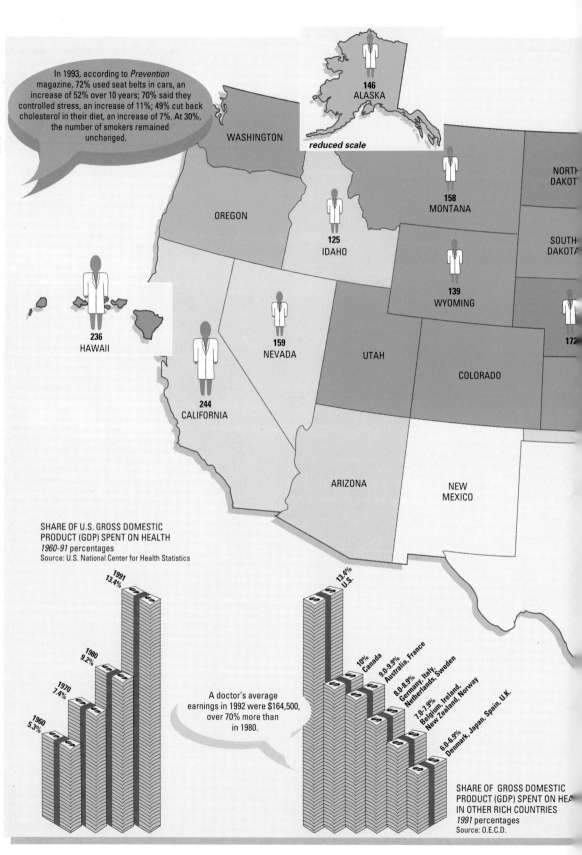

In 1993, according to *Prevention* magazine, 72% used seat belts in cars, an increase of 52% over 10 years; 70% said they controlled stress, an increase of 11%; 49% cut back cholesterol in their diet, an increase of 7%. At 30%, the number of smokers remained unchanged.

146 ALASKA
reduced scale

WASHINGTON

OREGON

158 MONTANA

125 IDAHO

139 WYOMING

NORTH DAKOT

SOUTH DAKOT

236 HAWAII

159 NEVADA

UTAH

COLORADO

172

244 CALIFORNIA

ARIZONA

NEW MEXICO

SHARE OF U.S. GROSS DOMESTIC PRODUCT (GDP) SPENT ON HEALTH
1960-91 percentages
Source: U.S. National Center for Health Statistics

1991 13.4%
1980 9.2%
1970 7.4%
1960 5.3%

A doctor's average earnings in 1992 were $164,500, over 70% more than in 1980.

13.4% U.S.
10% Canada
9.0-9.9% Australia, France
8.0-8.9% Germany, Italy, Netherlands, Sweden
7.0-7.9% Belgium, Ireland, New Zealand, Norway
6.0-6.9% Denmark, Japan, Spain, U.K.

SHARE OF GROSS DOMESTIC PRODUCT (GDP) SPENT ON HEA IN OTHER RICH COUNTRIES
1991 percentages
Source: O.E.C.D.

The U.S. spends more on health care than any other country in the world.

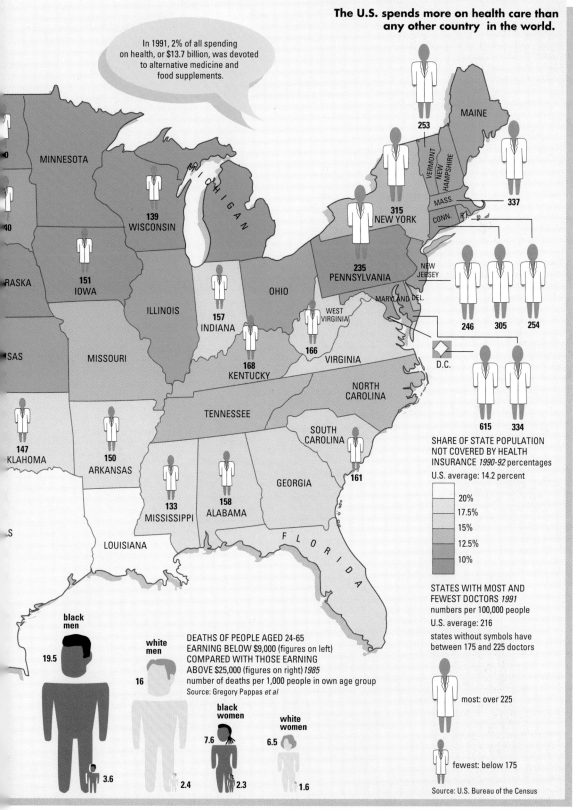

In 1991, 2% of all spending on health, or $13.7 billion, was devoted to alternative medicine and food supplements.

MAINE

253

VERMONT

NEW HAMPSHIRE

MASS.

337

315
NEW YORK

CONN. R.I.

235
PENNSYLVANIA

NEW JERSEY

MARYLAND DEL.

246   305   254

D.C.

615   334

MINNESOTA

MICHIGAN

139
WISCONSIN

151
IOWA

OHIO

157
INDIANA

166

WEST VIRGINIA

VIRGINIA

168
KENTUCKY

NORTH CAROLINA

ILLINOIS

MISSOURI

TENNESSEE

SOUTH CAROLINA

161

147
KLAHOMA

150
ARKANSAS

133
MISSISSIPPI

158
ALABAMA

GEORGIA

LOUISIANA

FLORIDA

RASKA

SAS

SHARE OF STATE POPULATION NOT COVERED BY HEALTH INSURANCE *1990-92* percentages

U.S. average: 14.2 percent

- 20%
- 17.5%
- 15%
- 12.5%
- 10%

STATES WITH MOST AND FEWEST DOCTORS *1991*
numbers per 100,000 people
U.S. average: 216

states without symbols have between 175 and 225 doctors

most: over 225

fewest: below 175

Source: U.S. Bureau of the Census

black men

19.5

white men

16

DEATHS OF PEOPLE AGED 24-65 EARNING BELOW $9,000 (figures on left) **COMPARED WITH THOSE EARNING ABOVE $25,000** (figures on right) *1985*
number of deaths per 1,000 people in own age group
Source: Gregory Pappas *et al*

black women

7.6

white women

6.5

3.6

2.4

2.3

1.6

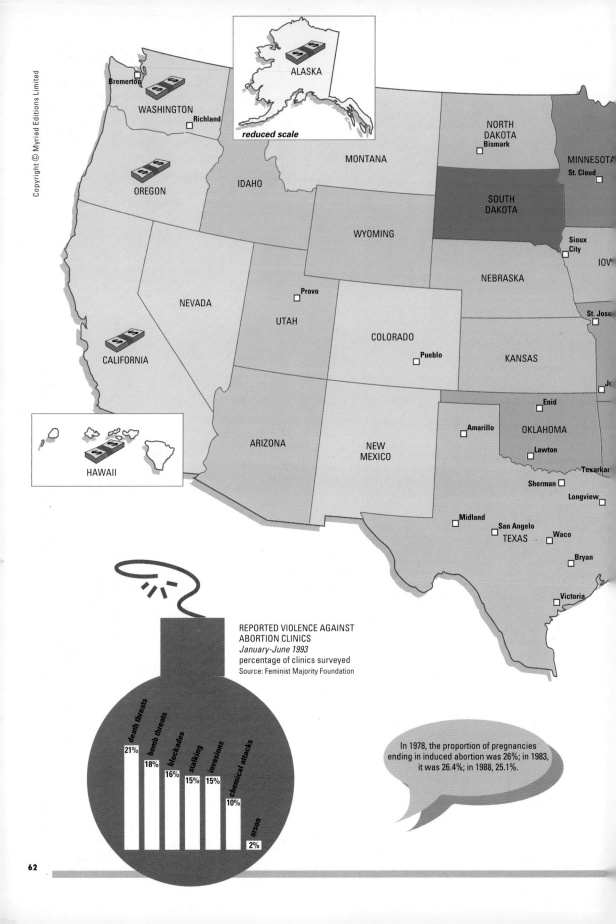

ALASKA
reduced scale

Bremerton
WASHINGTON
Richland

OREGON

IDAHO

MONTANA

NORTH
DAKOTA
Bismark

MINNESOTA
St. Cloud

SOUTH
DAKOTA

Sioux
City

IOW

WYOMING

NEBRASKA

NEVADA

Provo

UTAH

COLORADO

Pueblo

KANSAS

St. Jose

CALIFORNIA

Jo

Enid

Amarillo

OKLAHOMA

Lawton

Texarkan

ARIZONA

NEW
MEXICO

Sherman

Longview

Midland

San Angelo

Waco

TEXAS

Bryan

Victoria

HAWAII

REPORTED VIOLENCE AGAINST
ABORTION CLINICS
January-June 1993
percentage of clinics surveyed
Source: Feminist Majority Foundation

death threats 21%
bomb threats 18%
blockades 16%
stalking 15%
invasions 15%
chemical attacks 10%
arson 2%

In 1978, the proportion of pregnancies
ending in induced abortion was 26%; in 1983,
it was 26.4%; in 1988, 25.1%.

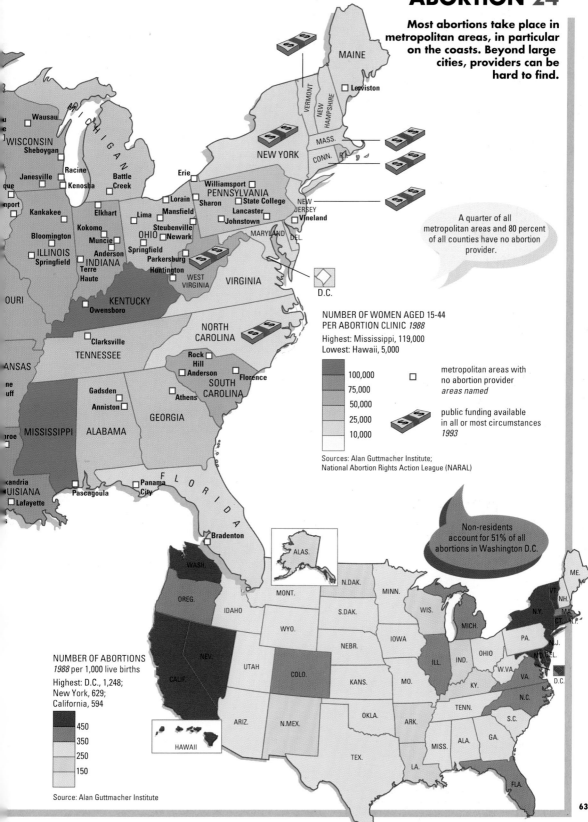

Most abortions take place in metropolitan areas, in particular on the coasts. Beyond large cities, providers can be hard to find.

MAINE

VERMONT

NEW HAMPSHIRE

☐ Lewiston

Wausau

MICHIGAN

WISCONSIN

Sheboygan

MASS.

NEW YORK

CONN.   R.I.

Racine

Janesville   Kenosha

Battle Creek

Erie

Williamsport ☐

PENNSYLVANIA

☐ State College

que

nport

Kankakee

Elkhart   Lima   Mansfield

Lorain   Sharon

Lancaster

Johnstown

NEW JERSEY

☐ Vineland

Kokomo

Bloomington   Muncie

Anderson

ILLINOIS   INDIA

Springfield   Terre

Haute

Steubenville

☐ Newark

OHIO

Springfield

Parkersburg

Huntington

MARYLAND   DEL.

WEST VIRGINIA

VIRGINIA

◇

D.C.

A quarter of all metropolitan areas and 80 percent of all counties have no abortion provider.

OURI

KENTUCKY

Owensboro

Clarksville

TENNESSEE

NORTH CAROLINA

NUMBER OF WOMEN AGED 15-44 PER ABORTION CLINIC *1988*

Highest: Mississippi, 119,000
Lowest: Hawaii, 5,000

ANSAS

ne

uff

Gadsden

Anniston ☐

Rock Hill ☐

☐ Anderson   ☐ Florence

SOUTH CAROLINA

Athens

GEORGIA

100,000	☐ metropolitan areas with no abortion provider *areas named*
75,000	
50,000	
25,000	💵 public funding available in all or most circumstances *1993*
10,000	

MISSISSIPPI   ALABAMA

roe

Sources: Alan Guttmacher Institute;
National Abortion Rights Action League (NARAL)

xandria

UISIANA

Lafayette

Pascagoula

☐ Panama City

FLORIDA

☐ Bradenton

Non-residents account for 51% of all abortions in Washington D.C.

ALAS.

WASH.   N.DAK.   MINN.

ME.

OREG.   MONT.   S.DAK.   WIS.   VT   N.H.

IDAHO   N.Y.   MA.   CT   R.I.

WYO.   MICH.   PA.

NEV.   NEBR.   IOWA   N.J.

OHIO   MD   DEL.

NUMBER OF ABORTIONS

1988 per 1,000 live births

Highest: D.C., 1,248;
New York, 629;
California, 594

UTAH   COLO.   ILL.   IND.   W.VA   VA.   D.C.

CALIF.   KANS.   MO.   KY.   N.C.

TENN.   S.C.

ARIZ.   N.MEX.   OKLA.   ARK.

HAWAII   MISS.   ALA.   GA.

TEX.   LA.

FLA.

450	
350	
250	
150	

Source: Alan Guttmacher Institute

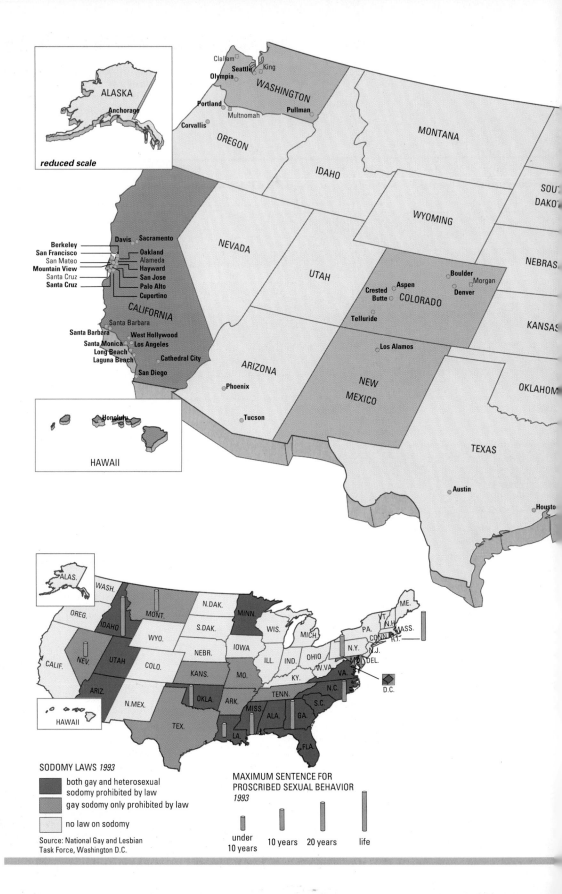

ALASKA
Anchorage
reduced scale

Clallam
Seattle   King
Olympia
WASHINGTON
Portland
Corvallis   Multnomah   Pullman

OREGON

MONTANA

IDAHO

WYOMING

Berkeley   Davis   Sacramento
San Francisco
San Mateo   Oakland
Mountain View   Alameda
Santa Cruz   Hayward
Santa Cruz   San Jose
              Palo Alto
              Cupertino

NEVADA

UTAH

COLORADO
Boulder   Morgan
Crested   Aspen   Denver
Butte
Telluride

SOUTH
DAKOTA

NEBRASKA

KANSAS

CALIFORNIA
Santa Barbara
Santa Barbara   West Hollywood
Santa Monica   Los Angeles
Long Beach
Laguna Beach   Cathedral City
San Diego

Phoenix

ARIZONA

Los Alamos

NEW
MEXICO

OKLAHOMA

Tucson

Honolulu

HAWAII

TEXAS

Austin

Houston

SODOMY LAWS *1993*

ALAS.
WASH.
OREG.
IDAHO   MONT.   N.DAK.   MINN.
         WYO.   S.DAK.   WIS.   MICH.   ME.
CALIF.   NEV.   UTAH   COLO.   NEBR.   IOWA   VT.   N.H.
                                                   ILL.   IND.   OHIO   PA.   MASS.
                  ARIZ.   N.MEX.   KANS.   MO.   N.Y.   CONN.   R.I.
                                    OKLA.   ARK.   KY.   W.VA.   N.J.
HAWAII   TEX.   LA.   MISS.   ALA.   TENN.   VA.   MD.   DEL.
                                                  GA.   N.C.
                                            FLA.   S.C.   D.C.

- both gay and heterosexual sodomy prohibited by law
- gay sodomy only prohibited by law
- no law on sodomy

MAXIMUM SENTENCE FOR
PROSCRIBED SEXUAL BEHAVIOR
1993

under   10 years   20 years   life
10 years

Source: National Gay and Lesbian
Task Force, Washington D.C.

Most Americans support civil rights for lesbians and gay men, who in many places have legal protection. But a backlash is brewing.

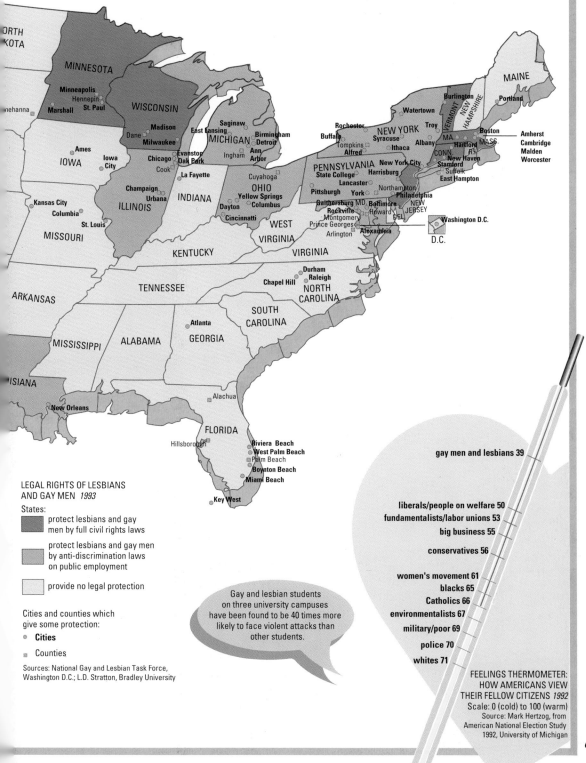

ORTH
KOTA

MINNESOTA
Minneapolis
Hennepin
Marshall   St. Paul
nehanna
WISCONSIN
Madison
Dane   East Lansing   Saginaw
MICHIGAN   Birmingham
Ames   Milwaukee   Detroit
Iowa   Chicago   Evanston   Ann
IOWA   City   Cook   Oak Park   Ingham   Arbor
Champaign   La Fayette   Cuyahoga
Kansas City   Urbana   INDIANA   OHIO
Columbia   ILLINOIS   Dayton   Yellow Springs
St. Louis   Cincinnatti   Columbus
MISSOURI   WEST
KENTUCKY   VIRGINIA
TENNESSEE
ARKANSAS
MISSISSIPPI   ALABAMA   GEORGIA   Atlanta

Watertown
Rochester   Troy
NEW YORK
Buffalo   Syracuse   Albany   Boston
Tompkins   Ithaca   Hartford   MASS.
Alfred   New Haven
PENNSYLVANIA   New York City   Stamford   Suffolk
State College   Harrisburg   East Hampton
Lancaster
Pittsburgh   York   Northampton
Gaithersburg MD.   Baltimore   Philadelphia
Rockville   Howard   NEW
Montgomery   DEL   JERSEY
Prince Georges   Washington D.C.
Arlington   Alexandria
D.C.

MAINE
Burlington   Portland
VERMONT   NEW HAMPSHIRE
Amherst
Cambridge
Malden
Worcester

VIRGINIA
Durham
Chapel Hill   Raleigh
NORTH
CAROLINA
SOUTH
CAROLINA

ISIANA
New Orleans   Alachua

FLORIDA
Hillsborough   Riviera Beach
West Palm Beach
Palm Beach
Boynton Beach
Miami Beach
Key West

LEGAL RIGHTS OF LESBIANS AND GAY MEN *1993*

States:

- protect lesbians and gay men by full civil rights laws
- protect lesbians and gay men by anti-discrimination laws on public employment
- provide no legal protection

Cities and counties which give some protection:

- **Cities**
- Counties

Sources: National Gay and Lesbian Task Force, Washington D.C.; L.D. Stratton, Bradley University

> Gay and lesbian students on three university campuses have been found to be 40 times more likely to face violent attacks than other students.

gay men and lesbians 39

liberals/people on welfare 50
fundamentalists/labor unions 53
big business 55

conservatives 56

women's movement 61
blacks 65
Catholics 66
environmentalists 67
military/poor 69
police 70
whites 71

FEELINGS THERMOMETER:
HOW AMERICANS VIEW
THEIR FELLOW CITIZENS *1992*
Scale: 0 (cold) to 100 (warm)
Source: Mark Hertzog, from
American National Election Study
1992, University of Michigan

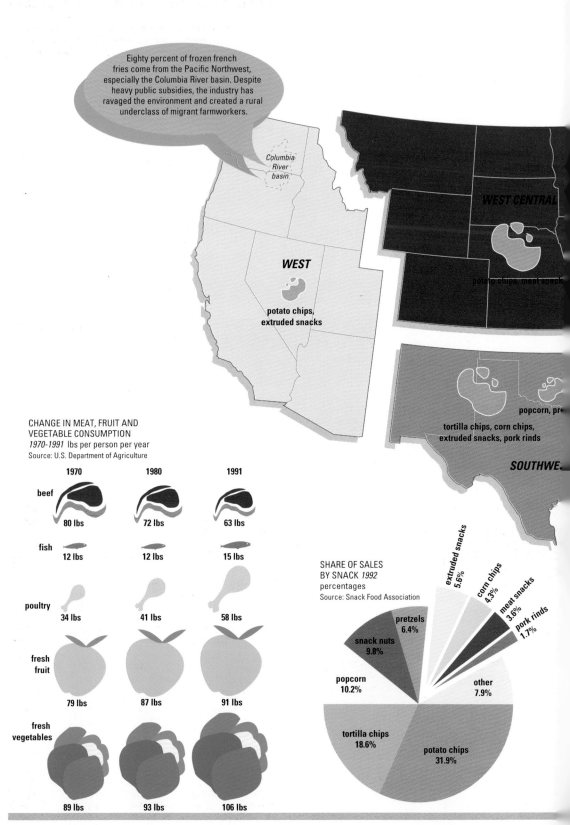

Eighty percent of frozen french fries come from the Pacific Northwest, especially the Columbia River basin. Despite heavy public subsidies, the industry has ravaged the environment and created a rural underclass of migrant farmworkers.

Columbia River basin

WEST CENTRAL

WEST

potato chips, meat snacks

potato chips, extruded snacks

popcorn, pr

tortilla chips, corn chips, extruded snacks, pork rinds

SOUTHWE.

CHANGE IN MEAT, FRUIT AND VEGETABLE CONSUMPTION
1970-1991 lbs per person per year
Source: U.S. Department of Agriculture

	1970	1980	1991
beef	80 lbs	72 lbs	63 lbs
fish	12 lbs	12 lbs	15 lbs
poultry	34 lbs	41 lbs	58 lbs
fresh fruit	79 lbs	87 lbs	91 lbs
fresh vegetables	89 lbs	93 lbs	106 lbs

SHARE OF SALES BY SNACK *1992*
percentages
Source: Snack Food Association

extruded snacks 5.6%
corn chips 4.3%
meat snacks 3.6%
pork rinds 1.7%
pretzels 6.4%
snack nuts 9.8%
popcorn 10.2%
other 7.9%
tortilla chips 18.6%
potato chips 31.9%

THE FAT OF THE LAND 26

Snack consumption – and obesity – continue to rise. Paradoxically Americans are also becoming more healthy.

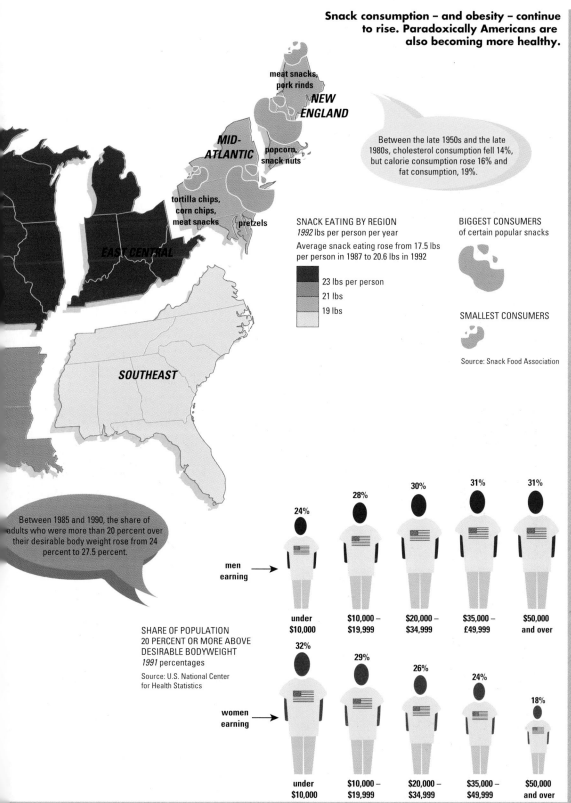

meat snacks, pork rinds

NEW ENGLAND

MID-ATLANTIC

popcorn, snack nuts

tortilla chips, corn chips, meat snacks

pretzels

EAST CENTRAL

SOUTHEAST

Between the late 1950s and the late 1980s, cholesterol consumption fell 14%, but calorie consumption rose 16% and fat consumption, 19%.

SNACK EATING BY REGION
1992 lbs per person per year

Average snack eating rose from 17.5 lbs per person in 1987 to 20.6 lbs in 1992

- 23 lbs per person
- 21 lbs
- 19 lbs

BIGGEST CONSUMERS
of certain popular snacks

SMALLEST CONSUMERS

Source: Snack Food Association

Between 1985 and 1990, the share of adults who were more than 20 percent over their desirable body weight rose from 24 percent to 27.5 percent.

men earning →

under $10,000	$10,000 – $19,999	$20,000 – $34,999	$35,000 – £49,999	$50,000 and over
24%	28%	30%	31%	31%

SHARE OF POPULATION 20 PERCENT OR MORE ABOVE DESIRABLE BODYWEIGHT
1991 percentages

Source: U.S. National Center for Health Statistics

women earning →

under $10,000	$10,000 – $19,999	$20,000 – $34,999	$35,000 – $49,999	$50,000 and over
32%	29%	26%	24%	18%

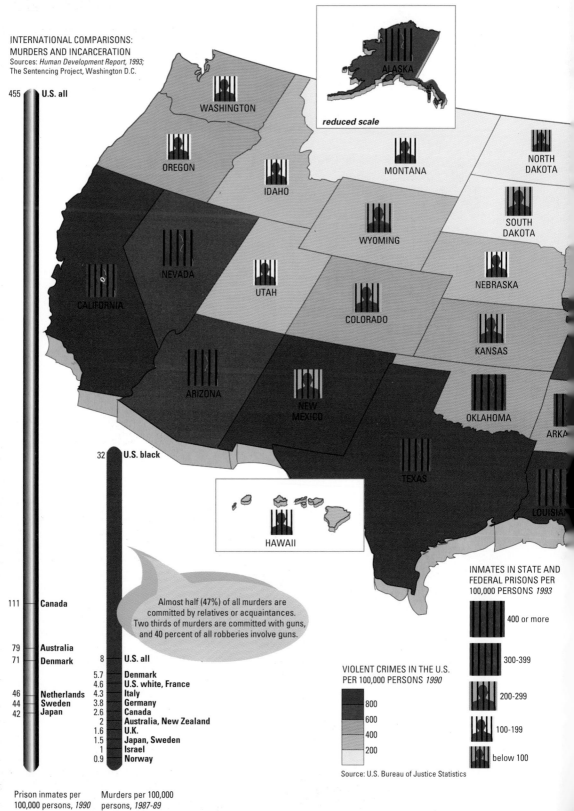

INTERNATIONAL COMPARISONS:
MURDERS AND INCARCERATION
Sources: *Human Development Report, 1993;*
The Sentencing Project, Washington D.C.

Copyright © Myriad Editions Limited

reduced scale

ALASKA

WASHINGTON

OREGON

IDAHO

MONTANA

NORTH DAKOTA

NEVADA

CALIFORNIA

UTAH

WYOMING

SOUTH DAKOTA

COLORADO

NEBRASKA

KANSAS

ARIZONA

NEW MEXICO

OKLAHOMA

ARKA

TEXAS

LOUISIA

HAWAII

455 **U.S. all**

32 **U.S. black**

Almost half (47%) of all murders are committed by relatives or acquaintances. Two thirds of murders are committed with guns, and 40 percent of all robberies involve guns.

111	**Canada**	
79	**Australia**	
71	**Denmark**	8 **U.S. all**
		5.7 **Denmark**
		4.6 **U.S. white, France**
46	**Netherlands**	4.3 **Italy**
44	**Sweden**	3.8 **Germany**
42	**Japan**	2.6 **Canada**
		2 **Australia, New Zealand**
		1.6 **U.K.**
		1.5 **Japan, Sweden**
		1 **Israel**
		0.9 **Norway**

Prison inmates per
100,000 persons, *1990*

Murders per 100,000
persons, *1987-89*

INMATES IN STATE AND
FEDERAL PRISONS PER
100,000 PERSONS *1993*

400 or more

300-399

200-299

100-199

below 100

VIOLENT CRIMES IN THE U.S.
PER 100,000 PERSONS *1990*

800
600
400
200

Source: U.S. Bureau of Justice Statistics

Between 1973 and 1993, the number of
[pr]ison inmates rose by 258 percent. The number
[of] all reported offenses rose by 42 percent, and
of violent crimes by 82 percent.

**The ranks of the imprisoned are growing
far faster than the crime rate. U.S. crime
and incarceration rates are the highest in
the industrial world.**

RACE OF MURDER
VICTIMS AND THEIR
MURDERERS *1991*
Source: U.S. Bureau of
Justice Statistics

92.7% of
victims of
black
murderers
are black

84.7% of
victims of
white
murderers
are white

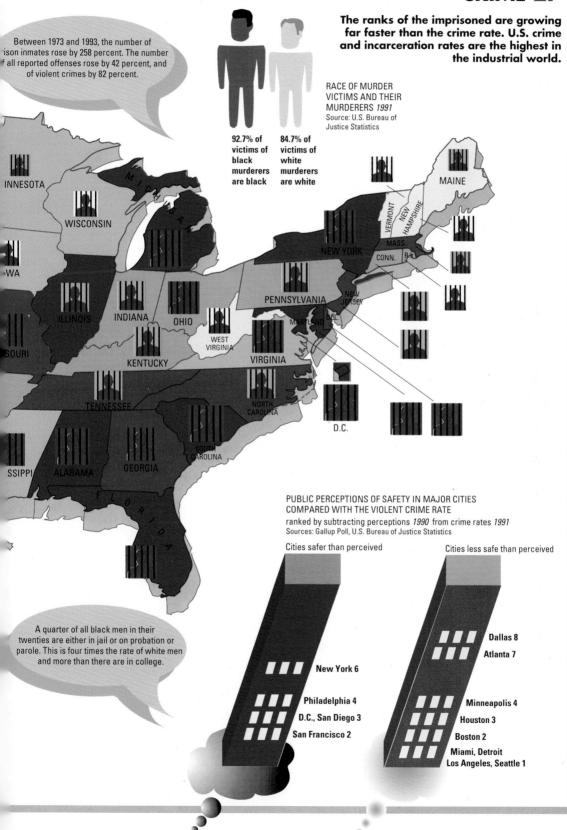

MINNESOTA

WISCONSIN

MICHIGAN

[IO]WA

ILLINOIS

INDIANA

OHIO

[MIS]SOURI

KENTUCKY

WEST
VIRGINIA

VIRGINIA

TENNESSEE

NORTH
CAROLINA

[MIS]SISSIPPI

ALABAMA

GEORGIA

SOUTH
CAROLINA

FLORIDA

MAINE

VERMONT

NEW
HAMPSHIRE

NEW YORK

MASS.

CONN.

R.I.

PENNSYLVANIA

NEW
JERSEY

MARYLAND

DEL.

D.C.

A quarter of all black men in their
twenties are either in jail or on probation or
parole. This is four times the rate of white men
and more than there are in college.

PUBLIC PERCEPTIONS OF SAFETY IN MAJOR CITIES
COMPARED WITH THE VIOLENT CRIME RATE
ranked by subtracting perceptions *1990* from crime rates *1991*
Sources: Gallup Poll, U.S. Bureau of Justice Statistics

Cities safer than perceived

Cities less safe than perceived

New York 6

Philadelphia 4
D.C., San Diego 3
San Francisco 2

Dallas 8
Atlanta 7

Minneapolis 4
Houston 3
Boston 2
Miami, Detroit
Los Angeles, Seattle 1

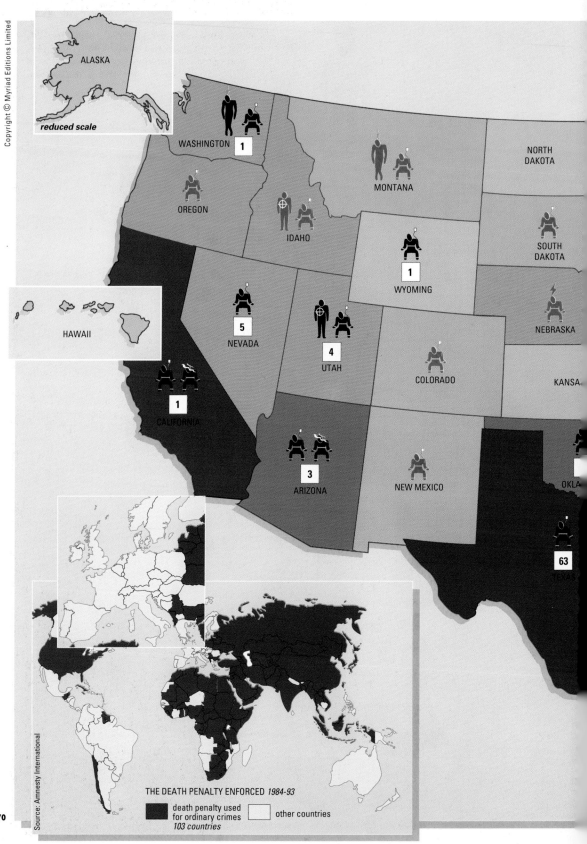

ALASKA

reduced scale

WASHINGTON **1**

NORTH
DAKOTA

OREGON

MONTANA

IDAHO

WYOMING **1**

SOUTH
DAKOTA

HAWAII

NEVADA **5**

UTAH **4**

COLORADO

NEBRASKA

KANSA

CALIFORNIA **1**

ARIZONA **3**

NEW MEXICO

OKLA

TEXA **63**

THE DEATH PENALTY ENFORCED *1984-93*

death penalty used
for ordinary crimes
103 countries   other countries

Source: Amnesty International

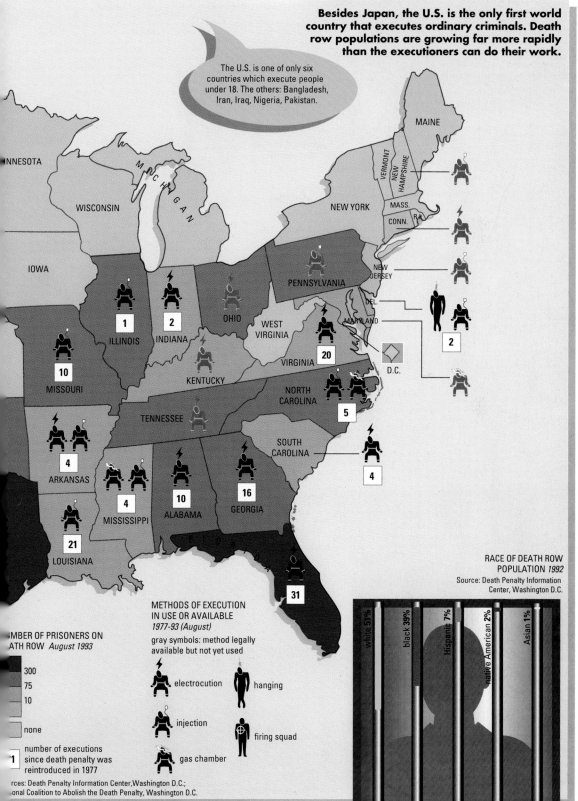

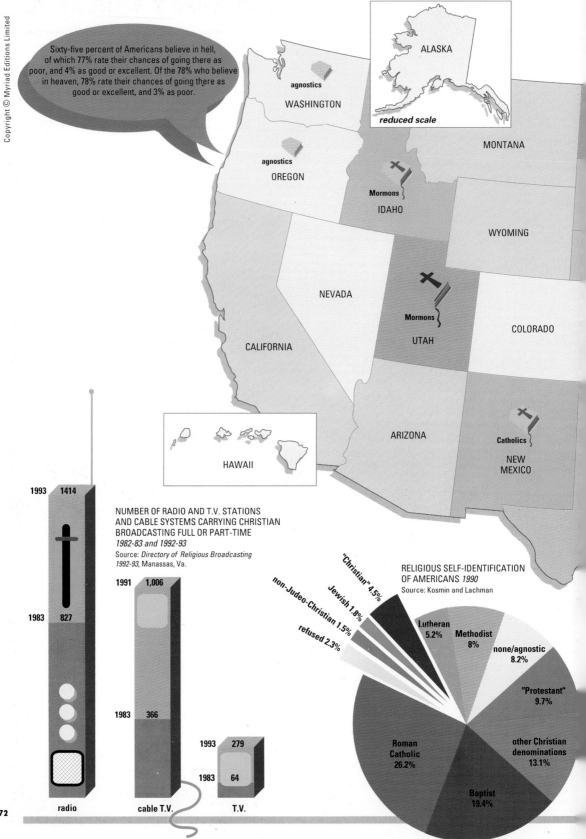

Sixty-five percent of Americans believe in hell, of which 77% rate their chances of going there as poor, and 4% as good or excellent. Of the 78% who believe in heaven, 78% rate their chances of going there as good or excellent, and 3% as poor.

ALASKA

reduced scale

agnostics

WASHINGTON

MONTANA

agnostics

OREGON

Mormons

IDAHO

WYOMING

NEVADA

Mormons

UTAH

COLORADO

CALIFORNIA

HAWAII

ARIZONA

Catholics

NEW MEXICO

1993 1414

1983 827

NUMBER OF RADIO AND T.V. STATIONS AND CABLE SYSTEMS CARRYING CHRISTIAN BROADCASTING FULL OR PART-TIME
1982-83 and 1992-93
Source: *Directory of Religious Broadcasting 1992-93*, Manassas, Va.

1991 1,006

1983 366

1993 279

1983 64

radio   cable T.V.   T.V.

"Christian" 4.5%

non-Judeo-Christian 1.5%

Jewish 1.8%

refused 2.3%

RELIGIOUS SELF-IDENTIFICATION OF AMERICANS *1990*
Source: Kosmin and Lachman

Lutheran 5.2%   Methodist 8%

none/agnostic 8.2%

"Protestant" 9.7%

other Christian denominations 13.1%

Roman Catholic 26.2%

Baptist 19.4%

**Six out of seven Americans are Christians.
Most religious diversity is Christian diversity.**

Catholics

Catholics

Catholics

MAINE

NORTH DAKOTA

olics Lutherans

Lutherans

MINNESOTA

Catholics

VERMONT

NEW HAMPSHIRE

Catholics

SOUTH AKOTA

Lutherans

WISCONSIN

Jews

MICHIGAN

NEW YORK

MASS.

CONN. R.I.

Catholics

Catholics

IOWA

NEBRASKA

INDIANA

OHIO

PENNSYLVANIA

Catholics

NEW JERSEY

Catholics

Catholics

ILLINOIS

WEST VIRGINIA

MARYLAND DEL.

Catholics

KANSAS

MISSOURI

KENTUCKY

Baptists

VIRGINIA

Baptists

D.C. Baptists

NORTH CAROLINA

Baptists

Baptists

TENNESSEE Baptists

SOUTH CAROLINA

Baptists

Baptists

OKLAHOMA

Baptists

ARKANSAS

Baptists

Baptists

Baptists

In 1986, a third of all adults
polled described themselves as
born-again or evangelical Christians.
By 1993, 45 percent did so.

Baptists

TEXAS

Catholics

MISSISSIPPI

ALABAMA

GEORGIA

LOUISIANA

F L O R I D A

**RELIGIOUS ADHERENTS
AS A PROPORTION OF
STATE POPULATIONS**
1990 percentages

70%

60%

50%

40%

no data

**STATES WITH LARGE SHARES OF
ADHERENTS TO AN INDIVIDUAL
RELIGION** *1990*

religions with adherents of more
than 1% of the U.S. population
Source: Kosmin and Lachman

not otherwise represented:

over 50% belong
to a single religion
named

over 30% belong
to a single religion
named

over 15% have
no religion or
are agnostic

over 5%
are Jews

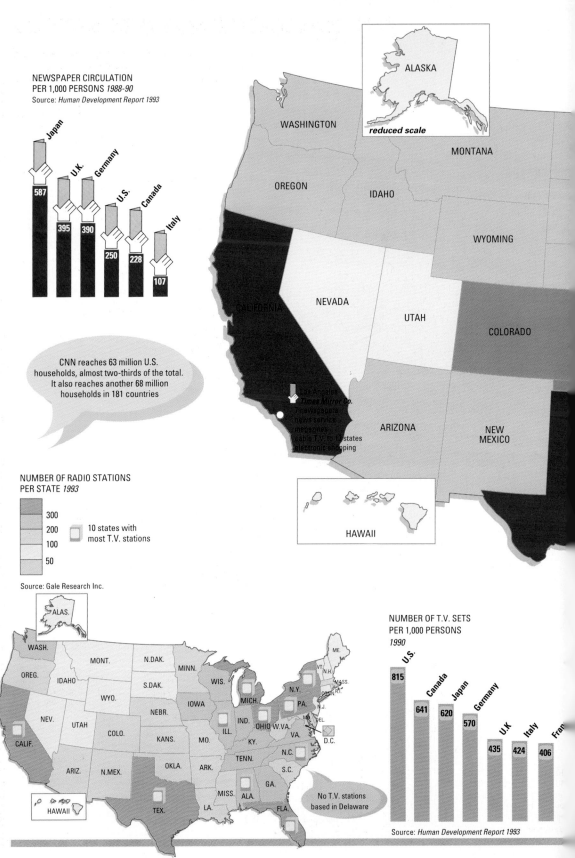

NEWSPAPER CIRCULATION
PER 1,000 PERSONS *1988-90*
Source: *Human Development Report 1993*

Japan 587
U.K. 395
Germany 390
U.S. 250
Canada 228
Italy 107

ALASKA
reduced scale

WASHINGTON
MONTANA
OREGON
IDAHO
WYOMING
CALIFORNIA
NEVADA
UTAH
COLORADO
ARIZONA
NEW MEXICO

CNN reaches 63 million U.S. households, almost two-thirds of the total. It also reaches another 68 million households in 181 countries

Los Angeles
Times Mirror Co.
7 newspapers
news service
magazines
cable T.V. to 13 states
electronic shopping

NUMBER OF RADIO STATIONS
PER STATE *1993*

300
200
100
50

10 states with most T.V. stations

Source: Gale Research Inc.

HAWAII

NUMBER OF T.V. SETS
PER 1,000 PERSONS
1990

U.S. 815
Canada 641
Japan 620
Germany 570
U.K 435
Italy 424
France 406

ALAS.
WASH.
OREG.
IDAHO
MONT.
N.DAK.
MINN.
S.DAK.
WIS.
WYO.
NEBR.
IOWA
MICH.
N.Y.
ME.
VT.
N.H.
MASS.
CONN. R.I.
NEV.
UTAH
COLO.
KANS.
MO.
ILL.
IND.
OHIO W.VA.
PA.
N.J.
MD. DEL.
VA.
D.C.
CALIF.
ARIZ.
N.MEX.
OKLA.
ARK.
KY.
TENN.
N.C.
S.C.
GA.
MISS. ALA.
TEX.
LA.
FLA.
HAWAII

No T.V. stations based in Delaware

Source: *Human Development Report 1993*

Copyright © Myriad Editions Limited

74

THE CONSCIOUSNESS INDUSTRY 30

U.S media ownership is slipping into fewer and fewer hands. Meanwhile the media companies are moving to a national, even global reach.

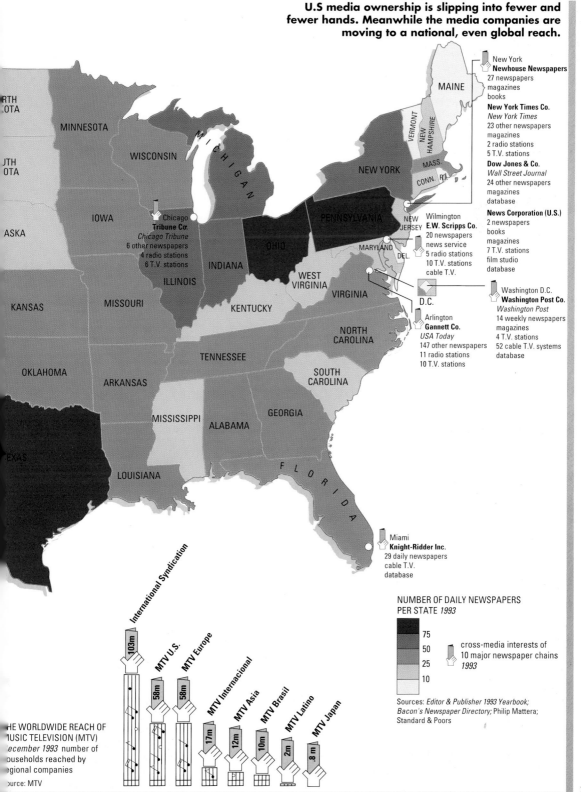

New York
Newhouse Newspapers
27 newspapers
magazines
books

New York Times Co.
New York Times
23 other newspapers
magazines
2 radio stations
5 T.V. stations

Dow Jones & Co.
Wall Street Journal
24 other newspapers
magazines
database

News Corporation (U.S.)
2 newspapers
books
magazines
7 T.V. stations
film studio
database

Wilmington
E.W. Scripps Co.
20 newspapers
news service
5 radio stations
10 T.V. stations
cable T.V.

Washington D.C.
Washington Post Co.
Washington Post
14 weekly newspapers
magazines
4 T.V. stations
52 cable T.V. systems
database

Arlington
Gannett Co.
USA Today
147 other newspapers
11 radio stations
10 T.V. stations

Chicago
Tribune Co.
Chicago Tribune
6 other newspapers
4 radio stations
6 T.V. stations

Miami
Knight-Ridder Inc.
29 daily newspapers
cable T.V.
database

NUMBER OF DAILY NEWSPAPERS PER STATE *1993*

75	cross-media interests of 10 major newspaper chains *1993*
50	
25	
10	

Sources: *Editor & Publisher 1993 Yearbook; Bacon's Newspaper Directory;* Philip Mattera; Standard & Poors

THE WORLDWIDE REACH OF MUSIC TELEVISION (MTV)
December 1993 number of households reached by regional companies
Source: MTV

International Syndication — 103m
MTV U.S. — 58m
MTV Europe — 58m
MTV Internacional — 17m
MTV Asia — 12m
MTV Brasil — 10m
MTV Latino — 2m
MTV Japan — .8 m

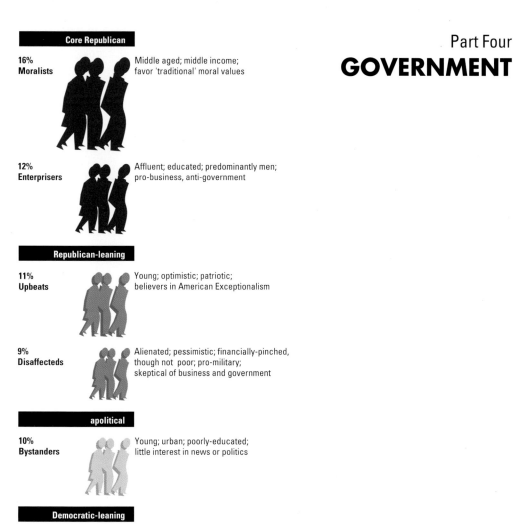

Core Republican

16%
Moralists

Middle aged; middle income;
favor 'traditional' moral values

12%
Enterprisers

Affluent; educated; predominantly men;
pro-business, anti-government

Republican-leaning

11%
Upbeats

Young; optimistic; patriotic;
believers in American Exceptionalism

9%
Disaffecteds

Alienated; pessimistic; financially-pinched,
though not poor; pro-military;
skeptical of business and government

apolitical

10%
Bystanders

Young; urban; poorly-educated;
little interest in news or politics

Democratic-leaning

9%
Seculars

Uniquely non-religious; some Republican sympathies;
believe strongly in personal freedom;
little interest in politics

Core Democrat

6%
New Dealers

Older; blue collar; financially comfortable;
religious; moderately hawkish;
intolerant on social issues

9%
60s Democrats

Well-educated; predominantly women;
tolerant on social issues; anti-military

17%
Pocketbook
Democrats

Average education; financially pinched;
concerned for social justice;
one-third are from "minorities"

Part Four
GOVERNMENT

A Times Mirror Political Typology *1992*
according to nine basic values and orientations

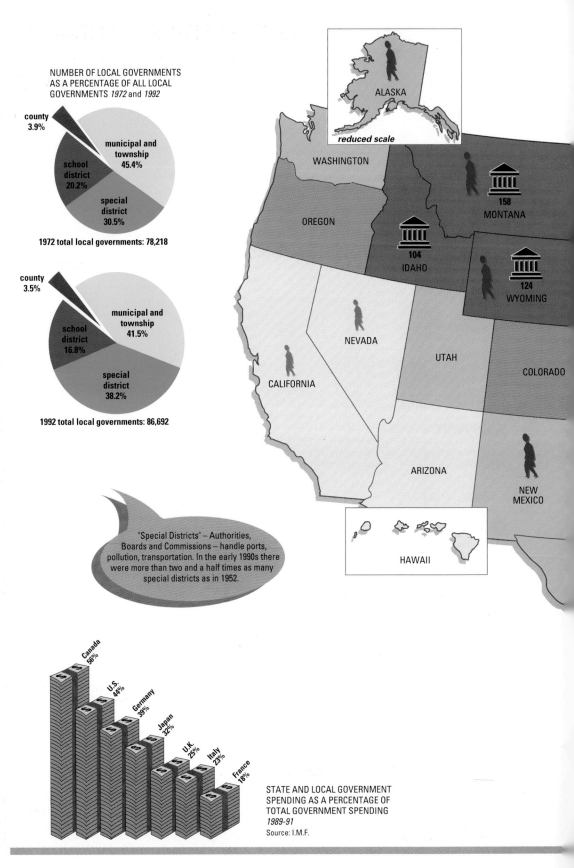

NUMBER OF LOCAL GOVERNMENTS
AS A PERCENTAGE OF ALL LOCAL
GOVERNMENTS *1972* and *1992*

county
3.9%

municipal and
township
45.4%

school
district
20.2%

special
district
30.5%

1972 total local governments: 78,218

county
3.5%

municipal and
township
41.5%

school
district
16.8%

special
district
38.2%

1992 total local governments: 86,692

"Special Districts" – Authorities,
Boards and Commissions – handle ports,
pollution, transportation. In the early 1990s there
were more than two and a half times as many
special districts as in 1952.

ALASKA
reduced scale

WASHINGTON

OREGON

MONTANA
158

IDAHO
104

WYOMING
124

NEVADA

UTAH

COLORADO

CALIFORNIA

ARIZONA

NEW
MEXICO

HAWAII

Canada
56%

U.S.
44%

Germany
39%

Japan
32%

U.K.
25%

Italy
23%

France
18%

STATE AND LOCAL GOVERNMENT
SPENDING AS A PERCENTAGE OF
TOTAL GOVERNMENT SPENDING
1989-91
Source: I.M.F.

78

There are more than 86,000 governments in the U.S., or one for every 3,000 Americans. Many are non-elected.

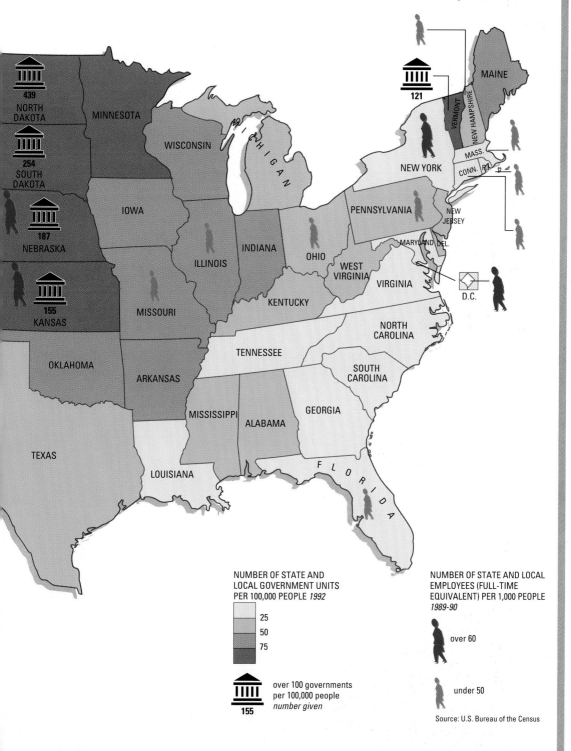

439
NORTH DAKOTA

254
SOUTH DAKOTA

187
NEBRASKA

155
KANSAS

121

MINNESOTA

WISCONSIN

MICHIGAN

MAINE

VERMONT

NEW HAMPSHIRE

NEW YORK

MASS.

CONN. R.I.

IOWA

INDIANA

OHIO

PENNSYLVANIA

NEW JERSEY

ILLINOIS

WEST VIRGINIA

VIRGINIA

MARYLAND DEL.

D.C.

MISSOURI

KENTUCKY

OKLAHOMA

ARKANSAS

TENNESSEE

NORTH CAROLINA

SOUTH CAROLINA

GEORGIA

MISSISSIPPI

ALABAMA

TEXAS

LOUISIANA

FLORIDA

NUMBER OF STATE AND LOCAL GOVERNMENT UNITS PER 100,000 PEOPLE *1992*

25
50
75

over 100 governments per 100,000 people *number given*

155

NUMBER OF STATE AND LOCAL EMPLOYEES (FULL-TIME EQUIVALENT) PER 1,000 PEOPLE *1989-90*

over 60

under 50

Source: U.S. Bureau of the Census

79

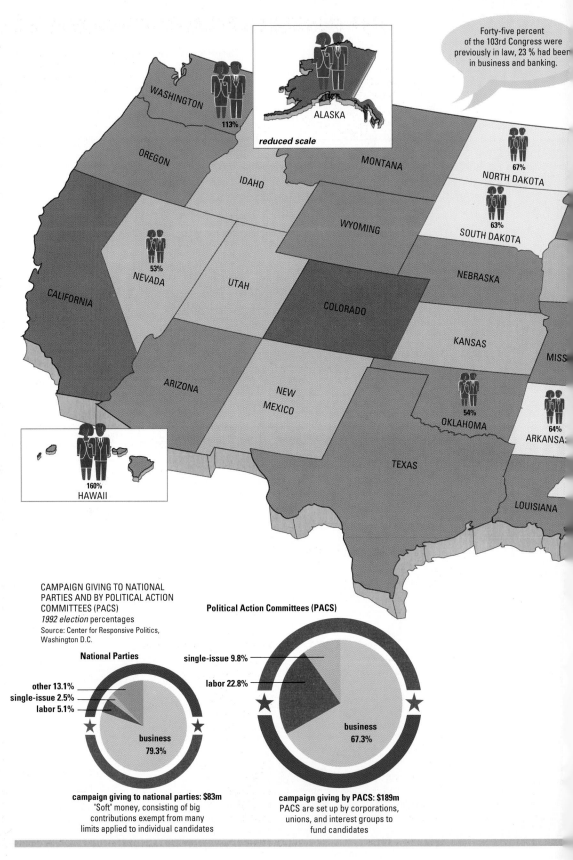

WASHINGTON
113%

ALASKA
reduced scale

Forty-five percent
of the 103rd Congress were
previously in law, 23 % had been
in business and banking.

OREGON

IDAHO

MONTANA

NORTH DAKOTA
67%

WYOMING

SOUTH DAKOTA
63%

NEVADA
53%

UTAH

COLORADO

NEBRASKA

CALIFORNIA

KANSAS

MISS

ARIZONA

NEW
MEXICO

OKLAHOMA
54%

ARKANSAS
64%

HAWAII
160%

TEXAS

LOUISIANA

CAMPAIGN GIVING TO NATIONAL
PARTIES AND BY POLITICAL ACTION
COMMITTEES (PACS)
1992 election percentages
Source: Center for Responsive Politics,
Washington D.C.

Political Action Committees (PACS)

National Parties

single-issue 9.8%

labor 22.8%

other 13.1%
single-issue 2.5%
labor 5.1%

business
79.3%

business
67.3%

campaign giving to national parties: $83m
"Soft" money, consisting of big
contributions exempt from many
limits applied to individual candidates

campaign giving by PACS: $189m
PACS are set up by corporations,
unions, and interest groups to
fund candidates

Presidents come and go, but the lawyers, lobbyists, and campaign contributors who make America run – the permanent government – are always with us.

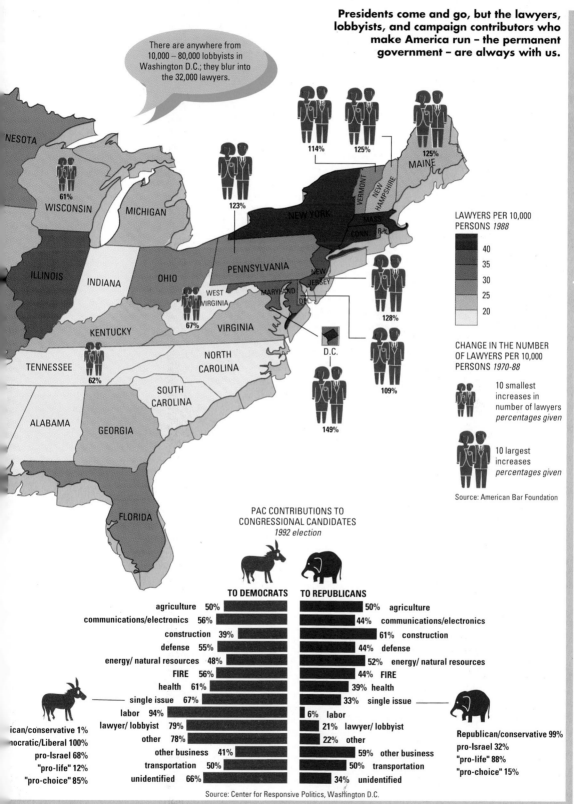

There are anywhere from 10,000 – 80,000 lobbyists in Washington D.C.; they blur into the 32,000 lawyers.

114%   125%   125% MAINE

123%

NEW YORK

VERMONT   NEW HAMPSHIRE

MASS.   CONN.   R.I.

PENNSYLVANIA

NEW JERSEY   128%

WEST VIRGINIA   67%   VIRGINIA

MARYLAND   DEL.

D.C.   109%

149%

WISCONSIN   61%

MINNESOTA   MICHIGAN

ILLINOIS   INDIANA   OHIO

KENTUCKY

TENNESSEE   62%

NORTH CAROLINA

SOUTH CAROLINA

ALABAMA   GEORGIA

FLORIDA

LAWYERS PER 10,000 PERSONS *1988*

- 40
- 35
- 30
- 25
- 20

CHANGE IN THE NUMBER OF LAWYERS PER 10,000 PERSONS *1970-88*

10 smallest increases in number of lawyers *percentages given*

10 largest increases *percentages given*

Source: American Bar Foundation

PAC CONTRIBUTIONS TO CONGRESSIONAL CANDIDATES
1992 election

TO DEMOCRATS		TO REPUBLICANS
agriculture	50%	50% agriculture
communications/electronics	56%	44% communications/electronics
construction	39%	61% construction
defense	55%	44% defense
energy/ natural resources	48%	52% energy/ natural resources
FIRE	56%	44% FIRE
health	61%	39% health
single issue	67%	33% single issue
labor	94%	6% labor
lawyer/ lobbyist	79%	21% lawyer/ lobbyist
other	78%	22% other
other business	41%	59% other business
transportation	50%	50% transportation
unidentified	66%	34% unidentified

Republican/conservative 1%
Democratic/Liberal 100%
pro-Israel 68%
"pro-life" 12%
"pro-choice" 85%

Republican/conservative 99%
pro-Israel 32%
"pro-life" 88%
"pro-choice" 15%

Source: Center for Responsive Politics, Washington D.C.

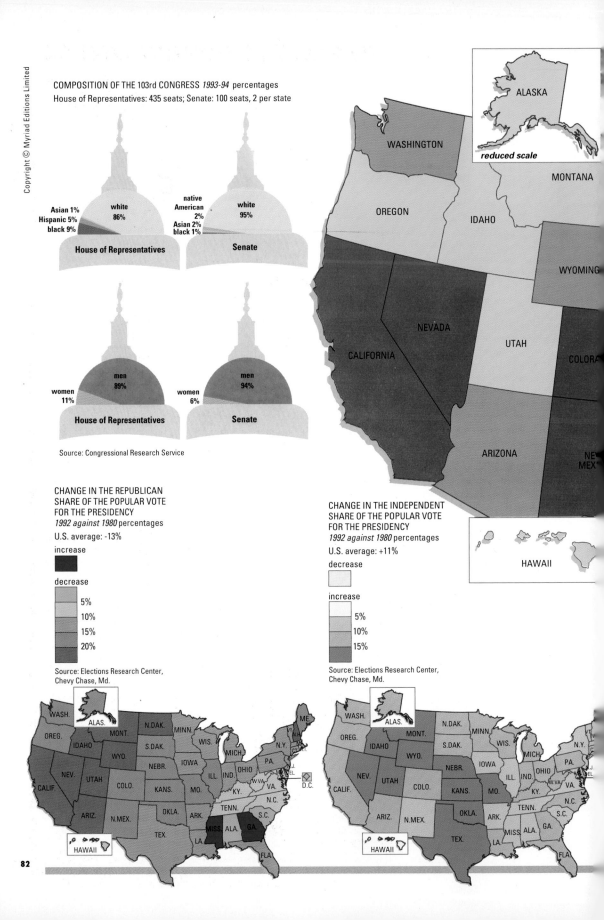

COMPOSITION OF THE 103rd CONGRESS *1993-94* percentages
House of Representatives: 435 seats; Senate: 100 seats, 2 per state

Asian 1%
Hispanic 5%
black 9%
white 86%

House of Representatives

native American 2%
Asian 2%
black 1%
white 95%

Senate

women 11%
men 89%

House of Representatives

women 6%
men 94%

Senate

Source: Congressional Research Service

CHANGE IN THE REPUBLICAN
SHARE OF THE POPULAR VOTE
FOR THE PRESIDENCY
1992 against 1980 percentages
U.S. average: -13%

increase

decrease
5%
10%
15%
20%

Source: Elections Research Center,
Chevy Chase, Md.

CHANGE IN THE INDEPENDENT
SHARE OF THE POPULAR VOTE
FOR THE PRESIDENCY
1992 against 1980 percentages
U.S. average: +11%

decrease

increase
5%
10%
15%

Source: Elections Research Center,
Chevy Chase, Md.

ALASKA
reduced scale

WASHINGTON
MONTANA
OREGON
IDAHO
WYOMING
NEVADA
UTAH
CALIFORNIA
COLORA
ARIZONA
NEW MEX

HAWAII

WASH. ALAS. N.DAK. MINN. ME.
OREG. MONT. WIS. N.Y.
IDAHO S.DAK. MICH.
WYO. PA.
NEV. NEBR. IOWA OHIO
ILL. IND. W.VA. VA. D.C.
CALIF. UTAH COLO. KANS. MO. KY.
N.C.
OKLA. TENN. S.C.
ARIZ. N.MEX. ARK.
MISS. ALA. GA.
TEX. LA.
HAWAII FLA.

WASH. ALAS. N.DAK. MINN.
OREG. MONT. WIS. N.Y.
IDAHO S.DAK. MICH.
WYO. PA.
NEV. NEBR. IOWA OHIO
ILL. IND. W.VA. VA.
CALIF. UTAH COLO. KANS. MO. KY.
N.C.
OKLA. TENN. S.C.
ARIZ. N.MEX. ARK.
MISS. ALA. GA.
TEX. LA.
HAWAII FLA.

Between 1980 and 1992, the average swing to the Democrats in Presidential elections was just 2 percent. The major gains were made by the independent candidate.

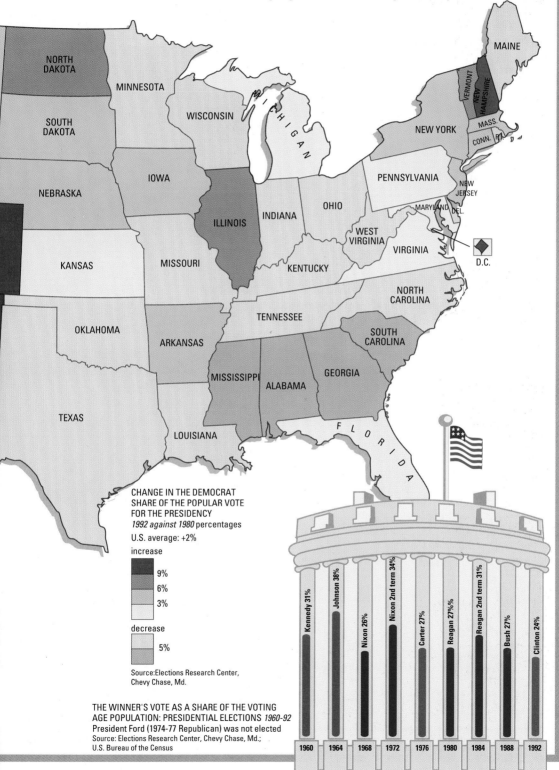

NORTH DAKOTA

MINNESOTA

SOUTH DAKOTA

WISCONSIN

MICHIGAN

MAINE

VERMONT

NEW HAMPSHIRE

NEW YORK

MASS.

CONN. R.I.

NEBRASKA

IOWA

PENNSYLVANIA

NEW JERSEY

ILLINOIS

INDIANA

OHIO

MARYLAND DEL.

KANSAS

MISSOURI

KENTUCKY

WEST VIRGINIA

VIRGINIA

D.C.

OKLAHOMA

ARKANSAS

TENNESSEE

NORTH CAROLINA

SOUTH CAROLINA

TEXAS

MISSISSIPPI

ALABAMA

GEORGIA

LOUISIANA

FLORIDA

CHANGE IN THE DEMOCRAT SHARE OF THE POPULAR VOTE FOR THE PRESIDENCY
1992 against 1980 percentages
U.S. average: +2%

increase

9%
6%
3%

decrease

5%

Source: Elections Research Center, Chevy Chase, Md.

THE WINNER'S VOTE AS A SHARE OF THE VOTING AGE POPULATION: PRESIDENTIAL ELECTIONS *1960-92*
President Ford (1974-77 Republican) was not elected
Source: Elections Research Center, Chevy Chase, Md.; U.S. Bureau of the Census

Kennedy 31%
Johnson 38%
Nixon 26%
Nixon 2nd term 34%
Carter 27%
Reagan 27%
Reagan 2nd term 31%
Bush 27%
Clinton 24%

1960 1964 1968 1972 1976 1980 1984 1988 1992

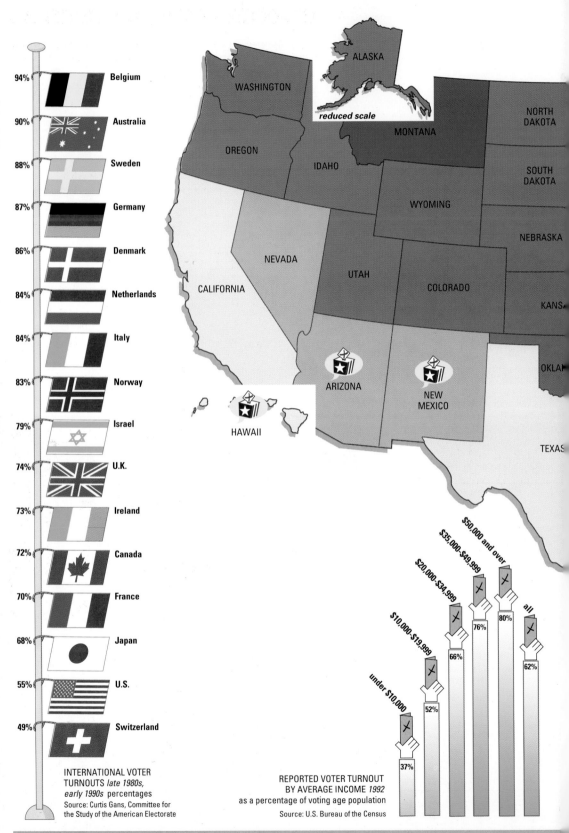

Copyright © Myriad Editions Limited

International voter turnouts (left flags):

- 94% Belgium
- 90% Australia
- 88% Sweden
- 87% Germany
- 86% Denmark
- 84% Netherlands
- 84% Italy
- 83% Norway
- 79% Israel
- 74% U.K.
- 73% Ireland
- 72% Canada
- 70% France
- 68% Japan
- 55% U.S.
- 49% Switzerland

INTERNATIONAL VOTER
TURNOUTS *late 1980s,
early 1990s* percentages
Source: Curtis Gans, Committee for
the Study of the American Electorate

Map labels:

ALASKA *reduced scale*

WASHINGTON, OREGON, IDAHO, MONTANA, NORTH DAKOTA, SOUTH DAKOTA, WYOMING, NEBRASKA, NEVADA, UTAH, COLORADO, KANSAS, CALIFORNIA, ARIZONA, NEW MEXICO, OKLAHOMA, TEXAS, HAWAII

Reported voter turnout by income:

- under $10,000 — 37%
- $10,000–$19,999 — 52%
- $20,000–$34,999 — 66%
- $35,000–$49,999 — 76%
- $50,000 and over — 80%
- all — 62%

REPORTED VOTER TURNOUT
BY AVERAGE INCOME *1992*
as a percentage of voting age population
Source: U.S. Bureau of the Census

84

The voting rate of Americans is one of the lowest in the rich world.

Ethnic group voting in 1992, as a percentage of voting age population:

Asian/Pacific Islander	27%
Hispanic	29%
black	54%
white	64%

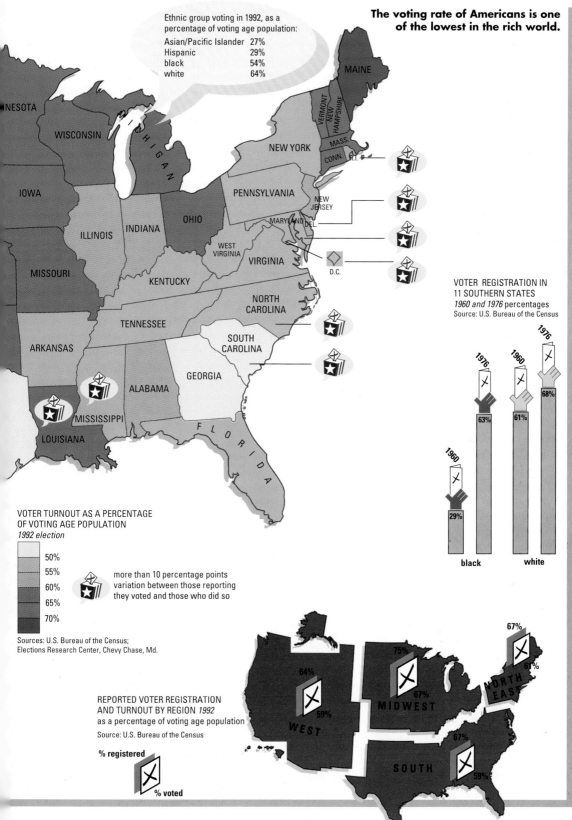

MINESOTA
WISCONSIN
MICHIGAN
IOWA
ILLINOIS
INDIANA
OHIO
MISSOURI
KENTUCKY
WEST VIRGINIA
VIRGINIA
TENNESSEE
NORTH CAROLINA
ARKANSAS
SOUTH CAROLINA
ALABAMA
GEORGIA
MISSISSIPPI
LOUISIANA
FLORIDA
MAINE
VERMONT
NEW HAMPSHIRE
NEW YORK
MASS.
CONN.
R.I.
PENNSYLVANIA
NEW JERSEY
MARYLAND
DEL.
D.C.

VOTER REGISTRATION IN 11 SOUTHERN STATES
1960 and 1976 percentages
Source: U.S. Bureau of the Census

black — 1960 29%, 1976 63%
white — 1960 61%, 1976 68%

VOTER TURNOUT AS A PERCENTAGE OF VOTING AGE POPULATION
1992 election

- 50%
- 55%
- 60%
- 65%
- 70%

more than 10 percentage points variation between those reporting they voted and those who did so

Sources: U.S. Bureau of the Census;
Elections Research Center, Chevy Chase, Md.

REPORTED VOTER REGISTRATION AND TURNOUT BY REGION *1992*
as a percentage of voting age population
Source: U.S. Bureau of the Census

% registered
% voted

WEST 64% / 59%
MIDWEST 75% / 67%
NORTHEAST 67% / 61%
SOUTH 67% / 59%

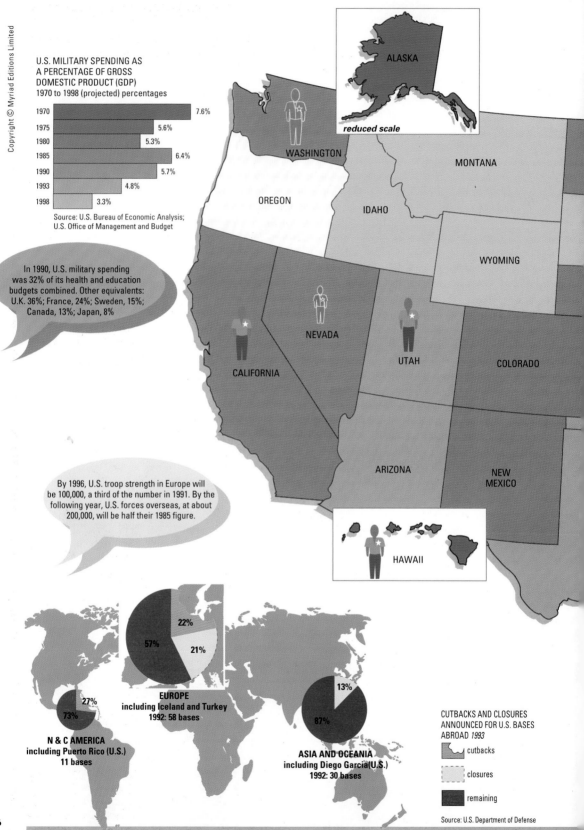

U.S. MILITARY SPENDING AS A PERCENTAGE OF GROSS DOMESTIC PRODUCT (GDP)
1970 to 1998 (projected) percentages

Year	Percentage
1970	7.6%
1975	5.6%
1980	5.3%
1985	6.4%
1990	5.7%
1993	4.8%
1998	3.3%

Source: U.S. Bureau of Economic Analysis;
U.S. Office of Management and Budget

In 1990, U.S. military spending was 32% of its health and education budgets combined. Other equivalents: U.K. 36%; France, 24%; Sweden, 15%; Canada, 13%; Japan, 8%

By 1996, U.S. troop strength in Europe will be 100,000, a third of the number in 1991. By the following year, U.S. forces overseas, at about 200,000, will be half their 1985 figure.

ALASKA
reduced scale

WASHINGTON
OREGON
MONTANA
IDAHO
WYOMING
NEVADA
UTAH
COLORADO
CALIFORNIA
ARIZONA
NEW MEXICO
HAWAII

N & C AMERICA
including Puerto Rico (U.S.)
11 bases
27%
73%

EUROPE
including Iceland and Turkey
1992: 58 bases
57%
22%
21%

ASIA AND OCEANIA
including Diego Garcia(U.S.)
1992: 30 bases
13%
87%

CUTBACKS AND CLOSURES ANNOUNCED FOR U.S. BASES ABROAD *1993*

- cutbacks
- closures
- remaining

Source: U.S. Department of Defense

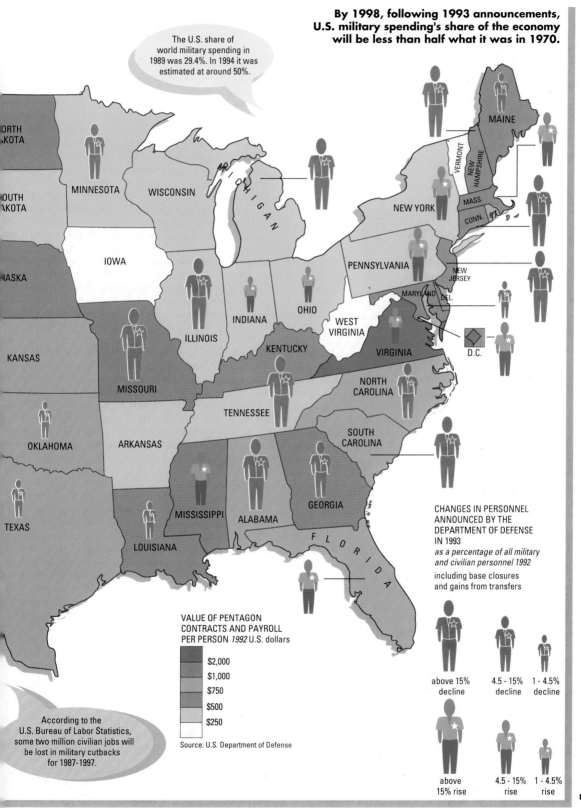

By 1998, following 1993 announcements, U.S. military spending's share of the economy will be less than half what it was in 1970.

The U.S. share of world military spending in 1989 was 29.4%. In 1994 it was estimated at around 50%.

CHANGES IN PERSONNEL ANNOUNCED BY THE DEPARTMENT OF DEFENSE IN 1993
as a percentage of all military and civilian personnel 1992

including base closures and gains from transfers

above 15% decline   4.5 - 15% decline   1 - 4.5% decline

above 15% rise   4.5 - 15% rise   1 - 4.5% rise

VALUE OF PENTAGON CONTRACTS AND PAYROLL PER PERSON *1992* U.S. dollars

$2,000
$1,000
$750
$500
$250

Source: U.S. Department of Defense

According to the U.S. Bureau of Labor Statistics, some two million civilian jobs will be lost in military cutbacks for 1987-1997.

State	1992 population		1990 shares of population		
	in thousands	% change from 1970	% foreign-born	% speaking language other than English	% who lived in different state in 19
U.S.A.	**255,082**	**+ 25.5**	**7.9**	**13.8**	**9.4**
Alabama	4,136	+ 20.1	1.1	2.9	8.7
Alaska	587	+ 95.7	4.5	12.1	21.3
Arizona	3,832	+116.4	7.6	20.8	19.3
Arkansas	2,399	+ 24.8	1.1	2.8	11.0
California	30,867	+ 54.7	21.7	31.5	7.2
Colorado	3,470	+ 57.2	4.3	10.5	15.3
Connecticut	3,281	+ 8.2	8.5	15.2	9.5
Delaware	689	+ 25.7	3.3	6.9	15.2
District of Columbia	589	− 22.2	9.7	12.5	19.1
Florida	13,488	+ 98.7	12.9	17.3	17.6
Georgia	6,751	+ 47.1	2.7	4.8	13.4
Hawaii	1,160	+ 50.8	14.7	24.8	16.3
Idaho	1,067	+ 49.6	2.9	6.4	14.8
Illinois	11,631	+ 4.7	8.3	14.2	6.3
Indiana	5,622	+ 9.0	1.7	4.8	8.4
Iowa	2,812	− 0.4	1.6	3.9	7.5
Kansas	2,523	+ 12.3	2.5	5.7	11.9
Kentucky	3,755	+ 16.7	0.9	2.5	8.1
Louisiana	4,287	+ 17.7	2.1	10.1	5.8
Maine	1,235	+ 24.5	3.0	9.2	11.6
Maryland	4,908	+ 25.1	6.6	8.9	12.0
Massachusetts	5,998	+ 5.4	9.5	15.2	7.9
Michigan	9,437	+ 6.3	3.8	6.6	5.5
Minnesota	4,480	+ 17.7	2.6	5.6	7.9
Mississippi	2,614	+ 17.9	0.8	2.8	8.1
Missouri	5,193	+ 11.0	1.6	3.8	9.4
Montana	824	+ 18.7	1.7	5.0	11.4
Nebraska	1,606	+ 8.3	1.8	4.8	9.7
Nevada	1,327	+171.4	8.7	13.2	29.4
New Hampshire	1,111	+ 50.5	3.7	8.7	18.7
New Jersey	7,789	+ 8.7	12.5	19.5	7.9
New Mexico	1,581	+ 55.6	5.3	35.5	13.9
New York	18,119	− 0.6	15.9	23.3	4.3
North Carolina	6,843	+ 34.7	1.7	3.9	12.1
North Dakota	636	+ 2.9	1.5	7.9	9.5
Ohio	11,016	+ 3.4	2.4	5.4	6.2
Oklahoma	3,212	+ 25.5	2.1	5.0	9.6
Oregon	2,977	+ 42.4	4.9	7.3	13.8
Pennsylvania	12,009	+ 1.8	3.1	7.3	6.3
Rhode Island	1,005	+ 6.1	9.5	17.0	11.3
South Carolina	3,603	+ 39.1	1.4	3.5	12.3
South Dakota	711	+ 6.8	1.1	6.5	10.8
Tennessee	5,024	+ 28.0	1.2	2.9	11.0
Texas	17,656	+ 57.7	9.0	25.4	7.5
Utah	1,813	+ 71.2	3.4	7.8	11.4
Vermont	570	+ 28.4	3.1	5.8	14.4
Virginia	6,377	+ 37.2	5.0	7.3	15.0
Washington	5,136	+ 50.7	6.6	9.0	13.9
West Virginia	1,812	+ 3.9	0.9	2.6	7.3
Wisconsin	5,007	+ 13.3	2.5	5.8	6.8
Wyoming	466	+ 40.4	1.7	5.7	14.9

Sources: Cols. 1 & 2: *as for map 1;* **Cols. 3 & 4:** *as for map 3;* **Col. 5:** *as for map 4;* **Cols. 6 to 10:** *as for map 2.*

STATE TABLE

% non-Hispanic white	% black	% Hispanic	% Asian/ Pacific Islander	% Native American/ Inuit/Aleut	State
		1990 shares of population			
75.6	12.1	9.0	2.9	0.8	U.S.A.
73.3	25.3	0.6	0.5	0.4	Alabama
73.9	4.1	3.2	3.6	15.6	Alaska
71.7	3.0	18.8	1.5	5.6	Arizona
82.2	15.9	0.8	0.5	0.5	Arkansas
57.2	7.4	25.8	9.6	0.8	California
80.7	4.0	12.9	1.8	0.8	Colorado
83.8	8.3	6.5	1.5	0.2	Connecticut
79.3	16.9	2.4	1.4	0.3	Delaware
27.4	65.8	5.4	1.8	0.2	District of Columbia
73.2	13.6	12.2	1.2	0.3	Florida
70.1	27.0	1.7	1.2	0.2	Georgia
31.4	2.5	7.3	61.8	0.5	Hawaii
92.2	0.3	5.3	0.9	1.4	Idaho
74.8	14.8	7.9	2.5	0.2	Illinois
89.6	7.8	1.8	0.7	0.2	Indiana
95.9	1.7	1.2	0.9	0.3	Iowa
88.4	5.8	3.8	1.3	0.9	Kansas
91.7	7.1	0.6	0.5	0.2	Kentucky
65.8	30.8	2.2	1.0	0.4	Louisiana
98.0	0.4	0.6	0.5	0.5	Maine
69.6	24.9	2.6	2.9	0.3	Maryland
87.8	5.0	4.8	2.4	0.2	Massachusetts
82.3	13.9	2.2	1.1	0.6	Michigan
93.7	2.2	1.2	1.8	1.1	Minnesota
63.1	35.6	0.6	0.5	0.3	Mississippi
86.9	10.7	1.2	0.8	0.4	Missouri
91.8	0.3	1.5	0.5	6.0	Montana
92.5	3.6	2.3	0.8	0.8	Nebraska
78.7	6.6	10.4	3.2	1.6	Nevada
97.3	0.6	1.0	0.8	0.2	New Hampshire
74.0	13.4	9.6	3.5	0.2	New Jersey
50.4	2.0	38.2	0.9	8.9	New Mexico
69.3	15.9	12.3	3.9	0.3	New York
75.0	22.0	1.2	0.8	1.2	North Carolina
94.2	0.6	0.7	0.5	4.1	North Dakota
87.1	10.6	1.3	0.8	0.2	Ohio
81.0	7.4	2.7	1.1	8.0	Oklahoma
90.8	1.6	4.0	2.4	1.4	Oregon
87.7	9.2	2.0	1.2	0.1	Pennsylvania
89.3	3.9	4.6	1.8	0.4	Rhode Island
68.5	29.8	0.9	0.6	0.2	South Carolina
91.2	0.5	0.8	0.4	7.3	South Dakota
82.6	16.0	0.7	0.7	0.2	Tennessee
60.6	11.9	25.5	1.9	0.4	Texas
91.2	0.7	4.9	1.9	1.4	Utah
98.1	0.3	0.7	0.6	0.3	Vermont
76.0	18.8	2.6	2.6	0.2	Virginia
86.7	3.1	4.4	4.3	1.7	Washington
95.8	3.1	0.5	0.4	0.1	West Virginia
91.3	5.0	1.9	1.1	0.8	Wisconsin
91.0	0.8	5.7	0.6	2.1	Wyoming

State	1990 shares of population			state/local taxes per $1,000 personal income
	urban %	suburban % (metropolitan, non-central city)	rural % (non-metropolitan)	
U.S.A.	—	—	—	141.3
Alabama	27.1	40.0	32.9	136.9
Alaska	41.1	0.0	58.9	249.0
Arizona	54.7	30.1	15.3	148.5
Arkansas	24.3	20.0	55.8	124.3
California	39.5	57.3	3.2	143.9
Colorado	35.5	46.1	18.5	138.4
Connecticut	28.6	67.1	4.2	123.1
Delaware	18.7	64.4	17.0	146.9
District of Columbia	100.0	0.0	0.0	191.8
Florida	24.5	68.4	7.1	128.9
Georgia	15.2	52.0	32.8	147.6
Hawaii	33.0	42.5	24.5	172.6
Idaho	15.3	14.1	70.6	144.9
Illinois	35.9	47.8	16.2	126.5
Indiana	31.2	40.3	28.5	134.8
Iowa	27.0	16.2	56.8	154.9
Kansas	29.9	23.9	46.2	138.1
Kentucky	17.0	31.3	51.7	132.6
Louisiana	30.6	44.3	25.1	153.1
Maine	13.2	22.9	63.9	142.0
Maryland	18.2	74.7	7.2	128.7
Massachusetts	32.6	63.6	3.8	127.2
Michigan	24.1	58.7	17.2	146.3
Minnesota	19.9	48.9	31.2	164.2
Mississippi	12.0	18.1	69.9	151.9
Missouri	23.6	44.6	31.8	116.1
Montana	17.1	6.9	76.1	149.8
Nebraska	33.4	16.4	50.1	152.9
Nevada	32.6	51.7	15.6	137.8
New Hampshire	20.9	38.5	40.6	102.2
New Jersey	12.4	87.6	0.0	123.7
New Mexico	33.2	22.4	44.4	158.9
New York	48.6	43.2	8.2	180.0
North Carolina	26.1	39.9	34.0	140.3
North Dakota	27.0	13.2	59.7	159.9
Ohio	28.7	52.7	18.6	134.5
Oklahoma	33.2	26.3	40.6	142.6
Oregon	26.9	42.9	30.2	152.8
Pennsylvania	23.7	61.2	15.1	124.5
Rhode Island	36.1	57.3	6.5	128.3
South Carolina	15.3	54.1	30.5	152.0
South Dakota	22.3	9.4	68.3	125.2
Tennessee	35.3	32.4	32.4	126.6
Texas	47.3	36.1	16.6	131.8
Utah	23.2	54.3	22.5	158.0
Vermont	7.0	20.0	73.1	148.6
Virginia	29.4	47.7	22.9	126.6
Washington	27.7	55.3	17.1	156.8
West Virginia	11.3	30.4	58.3	149.8
Wisconsin	32.5	35.6	31.9	156.9
Wyoming	21.3	8.3	70.4	187.9

Sources: Cols. 1–3: *as for map 6;* **Col 4:** *as for map 17;* **Col. 5:** *as for map 7;* **Col. 6:** *as for map 8;* **Col. 7:** *as for map 9;*
Col. 8: *as for map 14;* **Col. 9:** *as for map 15.*

STATE TABLE

1990 shares of gross state product			% of labor force in unions 1992	% of women in labor force 1992	State
manufacturing %	farming %	finance, insurance, real estate %			
18.9	**1.4**	**17.8**	**12.9**	**57.8**	**U.S.A.**
23.4	1.7	13.2	13.8	53.4	Alabama
3.9	0.1	14.0	20.8	65.7	Alaska
15.1	1.4	17.2	7.2	55.1	Arizona
25.3	4.2	13.4	8.6	55.4	Arkansas
16.3	1.4	20.3	18.2	56.0	California
13.9	1.8	16.9	10.1	62.6	Colorado
21.4	0.3	22.5	17.9	63.8	Connecticut
24.3	1.2	30.5	16.5	62.3	Delaware
3.5	0.0	13.2	13.4	61.7	District of Columbia
9.9	1.5	19.2	8.1	54.8	Florida
19.6	1.2	15.4	7.3	57.9	Georgia
3.8	1.2	19.5	28.6	61.9	Hawaii
16.3	8.2	18.6	9.2	59.2	Idaho
19.7	1.1	18.7	20.5	59.8	Illinois
30.5	1.8	13.9	19.2	57.5	Indiana
23.8	7.5	15.7	13.6	63.5	Iowa
19.5	3.8	14.8	11.5	62.8	Kansas
24.7	2.7	13.2	12.6	52.8	Kentucky
17.8	1.0	14.5	7.8	53.1	Louisiana
19.9	1.3	16.8	14.9	61.7	Maine
10.7	0.6	18.4	15.6	64.8	Maryland
19.2	0.2	20.5	17.0	60.0	Massachusetts
28.6	0.9	15.5	25.6	56.8	Michigan
22.1	3.5	16.7	22.2	65.7	Minnesota
24.4	2.6	13.8	9.1	53.1	Mississippi
21.8	1.6	15.4	13.8	60.0	Missouri
8.1	5.2	16.2	18.8	63.0	Montana
13.9	9.1	16.0	10.7	64.4	Nebraska
3.9	0.5	15.7	18.9	61.7	Nevada
23.3	0.4	19.7	9.8	64.9	New Hampshire
18.0	0.2	20.1	23.0	57.0	New Jersey
6.9	2.0	14.5	8.8	53.6	New Mexico
14.7	0.3	24.5	27.7	52.8	New York
30.3	1.9	13.3	4.8	60.8	North Carolina
6.7	9.3	17.4	9.4	60.1	North Dakota
28.0	0.9	15.3	20.4	57.1	Ohio
16.1	2.9	14.9	9.4	55.5	Oklahoma
20.2	2.7	16.1	18.6	59.3	Oregon
20.7	0.8	17.9	19.6	54.8	Pennsylvania
21.8	0.3	21.0	19.9	60.6	Rhode Island
26.1	0.8	13.1	4.9	58.8	South Carolina
9.2	12.6	21.3	8.9	62.4	South Dakota
23.8	1.1	14.4	10.4	55.6	Tennessee
17.4	1.3	15.6	6.9	59.2	Texas
15.5	1.3	15.0	9.6	61.0	Utah
21.1	2.0	17.7	10.6	66.0	Vermont
15.9	0.8	16.0	9.3	63.0	Virginia
19.7	1.9	16.5	23.5	60.7	Washington
16.0	0.8	13.2	18.4	43.7	West Virginia
29.0	3.0	16.1	19.9	64.8	Wisconsin
3.6	2.1	11.8	12.0	62.5	Wyoming

State	average 1990-92 shares of population		1990 infant mortality per 1,000 live births		
	% below poverty line	% without health insurance	all	white	black
U.S.A.	**13.5**	**14.2**	**9.2**	**7.7**	**17.0**
Alabama	18.4	17.3	10.8	8.3	15.9
Alaska	11.1	14.9	10.5	8.5	11.2
Arizona	14.5	15.8	8.8	8.2	16.7
Arkansas	18.1	17.6	9.2	8.0	13.6
California	15.1	19.0	7.9	7.6	14.2
Colorado	11.6	12.4	8.8	8.4	16.5
Connecticut	8.0	7.5	7.9	6.6	16.0
Delaware	7.3	12.7	10.1	7.3	19.4
District of Columbia	20.0	22.0	20.7	12.1	24.4
Florida	15.0	18.7	9.6	7.6	16.2
Georgia	16.9	16.1	12.4	9.1	18.0
Hawaii	9.9	6.8	6.7	5.1	11.5
Idaho	14.6	16.4	8.7	8.7	10.9
Illinois	14.2	11.8	10.7	7.7	21.5
Indiana	13.5	11.5	9.6	8.9	16.0
Iowa	10.4	9.0	8.1	7.8	18.0
Kansas	11.2	11.0	8.4	7.7	15.4
Kentucky	18.6	13.6	8.5	8.0	13.6
Louisiana	22.3	20.8	11.1	7.3	16.5
Maine	13.5	11.1	6.2	6.2	6.1
Maryland	10.2	12.3	9.5	6.5	16.3
Massachusetts	10.6	10.1	7.0	6.7	10.4
Michigan	14.0	9.4	10.7	7.9	21.0
Minnesota	12.6	8.8	7.3	6.7	19.7
Mississippi	24.6	19.3	12.1	8.5	16.1
Missouri	14.6	13.1	9.4	7.8	17.5
Montana	15.1	12.0	9.0	8.6	13.3
Nebraska	10.0	8.7	8.3	7.2	16.8
Nevada	11.9	19.3	8.4	8.1	12.5
New Hampshire	7.4	10.9	7.1	7.2	5.4
New Jersey	9.6	11.3	9.0	6.8	17.3
New Mexico	21.4	21.0	9.0	9.3	12.8
New York	15.0	12.6	9.6	7.7	17.3
North Carolina	14.4	14.2	10.6	8.3	16.0
North Dakota	13.4	7.4	8.0	7.9	—
Ohio	12.4	10.5	9.8	8.2	18.3
Oklahoma	17.0	19.5	9.2	9.4	13.2
Oregon	11.3	13.3	8.3	8.1	15.1
Pennsylvania	11.2	8.8	9.6	7.8	18.8
Rhode Island	10.0	10.2	8.1	8.3	9.7
South Carolina	17.2	15.4	11.7	8.3	17.1
South Dakota	14.0	12.2	10.1	8.6	7.4
Tennessee	16.5	13.6	10.3	8.0	17.5
Texas	17.1	21.9	8.1	7.1	13.9
Utah	10.1	11.5	7.5	7.4	13.0
Vermont	11.3	10.6	6.4	6.5	—
Virginia	10.1	15.5	10.2	7.5	18.8
Washington	9.8	10.7	7.8	7.6	14.5
West Virginia	19.4	15.0	9.9	9.6	16.6
Wisconsin	10.0	7.9	8.2	7.2	18.1
Wyoming	10.4	11.9	8.6	8.8	—

Sources: Col. 1: as for map 18; **Col. 2:** as for map 23; **Cols. 3–5:** as for map 19; **Col. 6:** as for map 23; **Cols. 7 & 8:** as for map 20; **Col. 9:** as for map 21; **Col. 10:** as for map 22.

STATE TABLE

doctors per 100,000 persons 1990	marriages per 1,000 persons 1988	divorces per 1,000 persons 1988	% over age 20, illiterate in English 1982	AIDS cases per 1,000 persons 1992-93	State
216	9.7	4.7	13	26.9	U.S.A.
158	10.9	5.8	13	16.1	Alabama
146	10.1	6.4	7	2.5	Alaska
197	10.2	7.4	12	28.2	Arizona
150	14.6	7.0	15	17.3	Arkansas
244	8.1	4.5	14	41.7	California
211	9.5	6.7	8	29.2	Colorado
305	8.6	3.7	12	26.3	Connecticut
199	8.6	4.6	11	38.3	Delaware
615	8.0	3.4	16	151.8	District of Columbia
208	11.2	6.4	15	56.2	Florida
175	10.9	5.5	14	33.6	Georgia
236	15.7	4.6	15	9.0	Hawaii
125	12.1	6.0	8	5.8	Idaho
212	6.7	4.0	14	20.5	Illinois
157	9.3	6.4	11	9.4	Indiana
151	8.9	3.8	10	7.3	Iowa
175	9.1	5.0	9	12.2	Kansas
168	13.3	5.4	15	6.6	Kentucky
188	7.7	—	16	21.3	Louisiana
178	10.4	5.0	11	6.2	Maine
334	10.2	3.6	12	30.8	Maryland
337	8.5	3.0	11	24.1	Massachusetts
185	8.2	4.3	11	12.8	Michigan
220	7.8	3.5	9	11.6	Minnesota
133	9.5	4.6	16	13.1	Mississippi
196	9.8	4.9	12	32.9	Missouri
158	8.4	5.1	8	3.8	Montana
172	7.6	3.9	9	8.4	Nebraska
159	111.3	13.2	9	32.4	Nevada
200	10.2	4.5	9	8.1	New Hampshire
246	7.9	3.5	14	37.4	New Jersey
183	8.4	5.5	14	17.0	New Mexico
315	8.8	3.5	16	60.9	New York
190	8.0	5.0	14	10.4	North Carolina
170	7.4	3.5	12	0.6	North Dakota
196	9.0	4.5	11	8.6	Ohio
147	10.2	7.1	11	18.5	Oklahoma
205	8.5	5.5	8	21.0	Oregon
235	7.3	3.2	12	13.9	Pennsylvania
254	8.5	3.8	15	16.3	Rhode Island
161	15.7	4.2	15	23.7	South Carolina
140	10.3	3.7	11	3.2	South Dakota
196	13.3	6.4	15	13.5	Tennessee
175	10.3	5.6	16	31.0	Texas
185	10.3	4.8	6	14.5	Utah
253	11.0	4.6	10	5.4	Vermont
213	11.5	4.3	13	18.8	Virginia
213	9.7	5.7	8	10.9	Washington
166	7.3	5.0	14	2.6	West Virginia
189	8.5	3.5	10	4.7	Wisconsin
139	9.9	6.9	7	7.1	Wyoming

State	abortions per 1,000 births 1988	1,000 women per abortion clinic 1988	violent crimes per 100,000 persons 1991	1992 units of government, all types	
				total	per 10,000 persons
U.S.A.	401	23	758	86,743	3.4
Alabama	282	48	844	1,134	2.7
Alaska	213	9	614	176	3.0
Arizona	348	28	671	598	1.6
Arkansas	180	52	593	1,473	6.1
California	594	11	1,090	4,495	1.5
Colorado	350	14	559	1,826	5.3
Connecticut	506	18	540	575	1.8
Delaware	498	17	714	281	4.1
District of Columbia	1,248	9	2,453	2	0.03
Florida	434	18	1,184	1,041	0.8
Georgia	331	29	738	1,321	2.0
Hawaii	574	5	242	21	0.2
Idaho	124	27	290	1,105	10.4
Illinois	392	53	1,039	6,810	5.9
Indiana	184	56	505	2,976	5.3
Iowa	252	39	303	1,904	6.8
Kansas	305	29	500	3,918	15.5
Kentucky	213	103	438	1,345	3.6
Louisiana	241	80	951	461	1.1
Maine	281	15	132	799	6.5
Maryland	462	22	956	416	0.8
Massachusetts	448	23	736	851	1.4
Michigan	442	28	803	2,727	2.9
Minnesota	279	80	316	3,616	8.1
Mississippi	122	119	389	898	3.4
Missouri	262	58	763	3,368	6.5
Montana	263	14	140	1,305	15.8
Nebraska	261	38	335	2,997	18.7
Nevada	554	12	677	212	1.6
New Hampshire	259	19	119	531	4.8
New Jersey	553	20	635	1,625	2.1
New Mexico	249	15	835	494	3.1
New York	629	14	1,164	3,319	1.8
North Carolina	389	16	658	954	1.4
North Dakota	197	45	65	2,795	43.9
Ohio	324	48	562	3,534	3.2
Oklahoma	255	57	584	1,882	5.7
Oregon	390	15	506	1,487	5.0
Pennsylvania	300	31	450	5,397	4.5
Rhode Island	477	38	462	128	1.3
South Carolina	257	56	973	705	2.0
South Dakota	81	175	182	1,803	25.4
Tennessee	290	28	726	960	1.9
Texas	331	45	840	4,919	2.8
Utah	138	49	287	635	3.5
Vermont	451	10	117	690	12.1
Virginia	382	20	373	461	0.7
Washington	471	17	523	1,796	3.5
West Virginia	140	67	191	708	3.9
Wisconsin	249	66	277	2,752	5.5
Wyoming	89	28	310	576	12.4

Sources: Cols. 1 & 2: *as for map 24;* **Col. 3:** *as for map 27;* **Cols. 4 & 5:** *as for map 31;* **Col. 6:** *as for map 34;* **Cols. 7–9:** *as for map 35.*

STATE TABLE

voter turnout, % of voting age population 1992	1992 military spending per person, $			State
	total	contracts	payroll	
55.2	829	440	389	U.S.A.
55.2	988	471	517	Alabama
65.6	2,677	655	2,022	Alaska
54.1	941	508	433	Arizona
53.8	414	120	294	Arkansas
49.1	1,231	772	460	California
62.7	1,345	713	632	Colorado
63.7	1.134	945	189	Connecticut
55.2	535	149	386	Delaware
49.7	4,834	2,643	2,191	District of Columbia
50.2	836	370	466	Florida
46.9	1,186	560	625	Georgia
42.0	2,565	539	2,026	Hawaii
65.1	334	62	272	Idaho
58.9	269	117	153	Illinois
55.2	462	268	194	Indiana
65.3	230	158	72	Iowa
63.0	810	340	470	Kansas
53.7	607	116	491	Kentucky
59.8	599	281	317	Louisiana
71.9	1,577	1,056	521	Maine
53.4	1,479	824	655	Maryland
60.2	1,114	949	166	Massachusetts
61.8	262	166	96	Michigan
71.6	415	335	80	Minnesota
52.8	1,394	982	413	Mississippi
62.0	1,028	715	312	Missouri
70.1	350	68	282	Montana
63.2	606	186	421	Nebraska
50.0	633	182	451	Nevada
63.1	577	380	196	New Hampshire
56.3	629	424	205	New Jersey
51.6	1,104	460	644	New Mexico
50.9	400	300	100	New York
50.1	816	225	591	North Carolina
67.2	748	230	517	North Dakota
60.6	473	275	198	Ohio
59.7	872	237	635	Oklahoma
65.7	215	69	145	Oregon
54.3	473	256	217	Pennsylvania
58.4	891	455	437	Rhode Island
45.0	959	210	749	South Carolina
66.9	476	117	359	South Dakota
52.4	447	251	196	Tennessee
49.1	887	490	397	Texas
65.1	920	340	580	Utah
67.6	243	110	133	Vermont
52.9	2,773	1,028	1,745	Virginia
59.9	1,074	431	643	Washington
50.7	159	46	113	West Virginia
69.0	267	179	88	Wisconsin
62.4	499	131	368	Wyoming

NOTES AND SOURCES

THE WORLD OF NUMBERS

Unlike many other countries, which have a single national statistical agency, the U.S. has a horde of them. It might be helpful to review the major ones. Within the Commerce Department are the Bureau of the Census and the Bureau of Economic Analysis (BEA). The Census Bureau not only conducts the eponymous national survey every 10 years; it collects enormous quantities of information on agriculture, industry, and state and local governments. It also does a detailed monthly poll called the Current Population Survey (CPS) that is the source of regular employment and unemployment data; the CPS is also the source of important data on income and poverty, health insurance coverage, household living arrangements, and union affiliation.

The BEA is the major producer of economic statistics, including the mother of all data series, the national income and product accounts (NIPA). NIPA's headline star is the gross domestic product (GDP), the total value of goods and services produced by land, labor, and capital located within the U.S. But GDP is the sum of many important details – production and spending of all sorts by households, businesses, and governments – all of which are reported in the NIPA. BEA publishes a monthly journal, the *Survey of Current Business*, that contains the latest NIPA reports and thousands of other economic and social statistics as well.

Numbers on work and prices are the province of the Bureau of Labor Statistics (BLS). It uses figures from the CPS to produce the monthly employment (and unemployment) report; it also surveys employers to produce figures on employment and pay. Its major publications are the *Monthly Labor Review* and *Employment and Earnings*, which are cited frequently throughout these notes.

Other agencies also have their own statistical operations. The Department of Agriculture covers food production and consumption; the National Center for Health Statistics, part of the Department of Health and Human Services, publishes figures on birth, death, and intervening events like marriage, divorce, reproduction, and illness. The Bureau of Justice Statistics, an agency of the Justice Department, pumps out reams of data on crime and punishment. And the Federal Reserve Board publishes numbers on money, banking, credit, and industrial producton.

Many of these statistics are now available at low or no cost to computer users. These electronic sources have been tapped wherever possible to produce this atlas. Among the most important are the Census Bureau's Cendata, available through Compuserve Information Service and the BEA's Economic Bulletin Board. These names appear in the sources wherever they were used.

Finally, trade associations, think tanks, academics, and interest groups also produce a gaggle of statistics, many of them based on raw government data. They will be noted and acknowledged in their place.

Part One
DEMOGRAPHICS

On the 1990 census Americans were asked to give their "ancestry or ethnic origin." Respondents were told to fill in a blank with up to two responses and were not supplied with a checklist. About 90 percent complied. Of that 90 percent, two-thirds reported a single ancestry group, and the remainder two groups. These raw answers were then classified into 215 standardized groupings. A little massaging of the data was necessary; "Cossacks" and "Muscovites" were slotted as Russian, for example.

About 5 percent specified "American" or "United States" as their nationality; just under 1 percent called themselves "white," "WASP" "Aryan," and what the Census Bureau calls other "other related groups." More than half of these two groups were Southerners. Only 1.4 percent gave "uncodeable" answers like "adopted," "don't know," and "none of your business." Answers specifying religions – many Jews, for example, consider that their ethnic identification – also had to be classified as uncodeable, since the Census Bureau is not allowed to collect information on religion.

Several changes are interesting in the reported ancestry between the Censuses for 1980 and 1990: the share of the population calling itself German rose, as did the share calling itself Acadian/Cajun or French Canadian, while that calling itself English fell. These shifts seem to have had more to do with the construction of the Census form than real changes in the population. In the 1990 survey, "German" was the first example of possible answers listed; not so in 1980. "English," was an example in 1980, but was dropped in 1990, while Cajun and French Canadian were added. The word "English" was further demoted in the sequence of questions: in 1980, respondents were asked if they spoke a language other than English at home before they were asked about ancestry; in 1990, the ancestry question was put before the language one. Such examples point to the power of human suggestibility and the ease with which surveys can be manipulated.

Source:
U.S. Bureau of the Census. *Detailed Ancestry Groups* (1990 Census of Population: Supplementary Reports 1990 CP-S-1-2, October 1992).

1 POPULATION

The cartogram shows that the northeastern states are still home to a large share of the U.S. population; but from the day the first white feet stepped on Plymouth Rock, the American population – natives excepted, of course – has been spreading southward and westward. The inset map shows that the center of population has persistently moved towards the south and west over the last two centuries and the colors given to states show that this trend continues still.

Though, on average, the U.S. population is young compared to other industrialized countries, and is likely to stay that way for the foreseeable future, it is graying as the baby boom ages. This resumes a trend that was interrupted in the immediate post-World War II years. In 1820, when living past 40 was fairly rare, the median age was just under 17 years (half the population being above the median age and half below). With the increase in life expectancy, the median rose steadily until 1950, when it reached 30 years. The baby boom, which lasted from 1946 to 1964, pushed it downward to 28 in 1970; but with the baby bust, the population's median age resumed its long-term climb, touching 33 years in 1990. The Census Bureau projects a further rise to 34 by 1995 and 39 by 2050.

An aging population requires more and more support. Will the working-age population be prosperous enough to finance the growing numbers of retirees? And will taxpayers be prepared to support them at more than subsistence level? These questions will become increasingly prominent in American politics as the millennium turns.

Sources to the map:
Day, Jennifer Cheeseman. "Population Projections of the United States, by Age, Sex, Race, and Hispanic Origin, 1993 to 2050." *Current Population Reports, 1993*: 25-1104. Washington, D.C.: U.S. Bureau of the Census, 1993; U.S. Bureau of the Census. Cendata computer database, through Compuserve Information Service, Columbus, Ohio.

2 THE MULTI-CULTURE

In most of the U.S.A., relations between Americans of African and European ancestry long constituted its most visible and complex inter-ethnic drama. Of course, indigenous populations belied that simple picture; even today, native Americans, including Inuit (or Eskimos), account for over 5 percent of the population in South Dakota, Oklahoma, Montana, New Mexico, Arizona, and Alaska.

Over the last few decades, race in America has become much more complex. Waves of non-European immigration, first from Latin America and the Caribbean and, more recently, from Asia have made not only social life more complicated – but language as well. It is standard to refer to everyone except non-Hispanic whites as "minorities," but in many areas, these "minorities" account for over half the population, and the Census Bureau projects that by 2050, only a little over half the population will be non-Hispanic white. It is not impossible to imagine that today's majority will, sometime in the next century, fall below half the population.

But there are further complexities. The Census Bureau, as well as common speech, uses the term "Hispanic" to refer to people who trace their ancestry to the Spanish-speaking countries of the Western hemisphere. (The Census Bureau is always careful to point out that Hispanics may be of any race and many Hispanics think of themselves as white.) But is using a single term to cover such a diverse population – a diversity illustrated on the inset map (bottom left) – justified? Many "Hispanics" chafe at the name officialdom has given them, preferring Latino (or Latina), while others want to be known only as Americans. The Asian-American population is also far more diverse than a single label allows.

Close-ups of the "minority" population for six representative states – counting D.C. as a state – are shown to get a feel for some regional differences. Mississippi, for instance, is representative of the Deep South, where black Americans are the predominant non-white group. Texas and Florida, by contrast, have large Hispanic populations – but Hispanics in Texas are predominantly of Mexican origin, while Cuban-Americans are prominent in Florida. California is a virtual United Nations to itself, with 43 percent of its population consisting of "minorities" by the conventional definition.

State, or even metropolitan area, maps are unable to convey an important point, however. A variety of ethnic groups live within the same borders, but this does not mean they live in the same neighborhoods, much less the same households. Though schools and workplaces may be meeting places for the multi-culture, many cities remain profoundly segregated residentially. Another measure of persisting segregation at a local level is that in the early 1990s only 2.2 percent of all marriages involve partners of a different race – three times as many as 1970, but still a very small share. Hispanics are more likely to marry non-Hispanics, however; marriages between Hispanics and non-Hispanics are over a third as numerous as those in which both partners are Hispanic.

Sources to the map:
Day, Jennifer Cheeseman. "Population Projections of the United States, by Age, Sex, Race, and Hispanic Origin, 1993 to 2050." *Current Population Reports*, 1993: 25-1104. Washington, D.C.: U.S.Bureau of the Census, 1993; U.S. Bureau of the Census. Cendata computer database, through Compuserve Information Service, Columbus, Ohio; U.S. Bureau of the Census. 1990 *Census of Population: General Population Characteristics* (1990 CP-1-1, November 1992) Washington, D.C., 1992.

3 WORLD NATION

For most of the 19th and early 20th centuries, over 80 percent of immigrants to the U.S., excluding Africans who came here in chains, came from Europe – first from the north and west, and later from the south and east. To those Americans of British and German extraction who were already here, the influx of Italians, Russians, and Poles seemed exotic, even threatening, at the time; the newcomers carried strange baggage, like a taste for garlic and socialism. That history now seems quite distant, as time, intermarriage, and assimilation to American cultural norms have heavily obscured the varieties of European-ness.

Now, despite the statistical blip resulting from the collapse of the U.S.S.R. and associated regimes, only one in ten immigrants into the U.S. comes from Europe. Nearly six in ten now come from the Western hemisphere, with most of the balance coming from Asia. Immigrants from Africa are few. These are the figures for legal immigrants only. Despite over a million expulsions of officially unwelcome migrants every year – and a total of nearly 30 million people over the last 70 years – the U.S. Immigration and Naturalization Service estimates that more than three million people live here illegally, mainly from Latin America.

As with race, language issues are sensitive. The most common term for foreign-born without official welcome is illegal aliens, but "alien" has extraterrestrial connotations. The most politically-correct term is undocumented immigrants, which, though it falls more gently on the ears, does obscure the fact that the full power of the state may be deployed against their continued residence. We have opted for "illegal immigrants".

Newly-arrived immigrants enjoy very different standards of living. On balance, the for- eign-born population is poorer than the native-born but, as usual, the averages hide the contrasting performances of individual groups. Those who have only been in the U.S. for a short time are poorer than those who are well-established. Those from northern and western Europe have incomes higher (and poverty rates lower) than the national aver- age, while those from eastern Europe and the republics of the former U.S.S.R. are, on average, poorer than the general population. Asians, especially Indians and Filipinos, also prosper, while those from the Western hemisphere tend to be poorer.

An interesting sidelight to the immigration story – the emigration story. It is popularly believed that once here, few people leave, but over the long term about a third of all immigrants do so. No official statistics on the matter exist, but according to State Department estimates, about 2.5 million American citizens live abroad, and the number is growing steadily. The government has not displayed much interest in collecting hard data because of its negative image.

Sources to the map:
U.S. Bureau of the Census. *The Foreign-Born Population* (1990 CP-3-1, July 1993) Washington, D.C., 1993; U.S. Bureau of the Census. Cendata computer database, through Compuserve Information Service, Columbus, Ohio; U.S. Bureau of the Census.*Statistical Abstract of the United States:1993*. Washington, D.C., 1993; U.S. Immigration and Naturalization Service Statistical Yearbook. Washington, D.C., 1991; U.S. Immigration and Naturalization Service. *Fact Book*. Washington, D.C., 1993; Warren, Robert and Ellen Percy Kraly. "The Elusive Exodus: Emigration from the United States." Population Reference Bureau. Population Trends and Public Policy, no. 8 (March 1985); Woodrow, Karen A. "Using Census and Survey Data to Measure Undocumented Immigration and Emigration from the United States." *Statistical Journal of the United Nations*, no. 7 (1990): 241–251.

Acknowledgment:
Maryann Belanger, Librarian at the Office of Population Research, Princeton University, Princeton, New Jersey for research- ing emigration from the United States.

4 ELBOW ROOM

In 1993, the U.S. population density averaged 73 persons per square mile, a figure not conducive to Malthusian nightmares of overpopulation. The U.S. is about a quarter as densely peopled as France, an eighth as packed as Germany, and less than a tenth as squeezed as Japan. And unlike Japan, much of which is uninhabitable, almost all the American land area is amenable to settlement. Canada is somewhat less densely popu- lated than the U.S., but that statistic is misleading, since most Canadians live in the southern part of the country, leaving the northern expanse very thinly peopled.

Within the U.S., too, there exist some strong regional variations. New Jersey, the most densely populated state, is about as thickly settled as the Netherlands. But next to Singapore, which is 10 times as densely populated, there is still plenty of room for New Jerseyans to stretch out. The New York metropolitan area (the city and its major sub- urbs), the country's densest conurbation, is a veritable open space compared to many of the world's major cities. Only Greater London is less densely populated than New York and its environs. But few cities in the northern hemisphere can compare to the density of Third World cities, which get more crowded every day as ambitious and/or displaced peasants migrate to town in search of employment.

The luxury of space may allow Americans to live largely but it exacts a heavy environ- mental price. Many Americans not only live in big houses that need to be heated in win- ter and cooled in summer, they also drive long distances to work or the shopping cen- ter.

Sources to the map:
U.S. Bureau of the Census. *Statistical Abstract of the United States:1993*. Washington, D.C., 1993.

5 ON THE MOVE

With industrialization societies grow more mobile, as people move from the country to the city. As in Europe a century or two ago, this pattern can now be seen throughout the Third World. But with time, it seems that industrial societies may settle down.

The new settler's length of journey is apparently a strong influence. It seems quite appropriate that people who have traveled thousands of miles to settle in the U.S., and not long ago on any historical scale, should continue to be mobile for years to follow. This explanation for American restlessness is confirmed by comparative statistics that show other "settler" countries (New Zealand, Canada, and Australia) with similar moving rates to U.S. figures.

Regional differences within the U.S. offer an interesting shading to this analysis. While the older states of the Northeast have suffered a long-term drain of population to the south and west (**1 Population**), they nonetheless show rather low levels of internal mobility. Over the five-year period from 1985 to 1990, 61 percent of Northeasterners remained in the same house, compared to 45 percent of Westerners. This suggests that as cultures age, mobility reduces too – a hypothesis supported by relatively low moving rates in Western Europe and Japan. This could be seen as a sign of torpor, or it could be argued that restlessness is something to be outgrown, as family and community ties deepen with time.

One hypothesis that can be discarded on the basis of research conducted by Larry Long, a U.S. Census Bureau demographer, is that a country's size influences the mobility of its population. Long examined 16 countries with good data, and found only a loose correlation between size and mobility. Long offers several other reasons to explain mobility – notably the degree of regulation of national housing markets and the relative expense of land and construction. Using regulation to explain mobility, however, may reverse cause and effect; a population that wants to move easily about will produce a loosely regulated housing market.

California, once a magnet for the migratory, is experiencing a significant human outflow for possibly the first time in history. As the inset map shows, the favorite destinations for people leaving California are the neighboring states of Arizona, Nevada, Oregon, and Washington. These numbers come from drivers' license changes, which means they cover only adult drivers moving from elsewhere within the U.S. Nearly everyone in California drives, so this is a reasonable measure. But it excludes children and, more important, immigration from outside the U.S., which is still strong (see inset map to **3 World Nation**.) In fiscal year 1992, nearly a quarter-million immigrants entered California legally, over half of these from Asia. Illegal immigration, especially from Mexico, is also significant. Unfortunately, illegal immigrants are unpopular and this is one of the many reasons that native-born Americans are leaving the state. There are others, many of which are similar to those given by people leaving New York City during its mid-1970s fiscal crisis – taxes, crime, congestion, deteriorating public services, and ecological crisis (though that last term was not in wide use in 1975). Eventually new areas become similarly afflicted and the cycle continues. As Adam Smith said, there's a lot of ruin in a country, and the U.S. is a very big country.

Sources to the map:

Long, Larry. "Residential Mobility Differences Among Developed Countries." *International Regional Science Review*, no. 14 (1991): 133–147; Long, Larry. "Changing Residence: Comparative Perspectives on its Relationship to Age, Sex, and Marital Status." *Population Studies*, no. 46 (1992):141–158; U.S. Bureau of the Census. *Statistical Abstract of the United States:1993.* Washington, D.C., 1993.

Acknowledgments:

Elizabeth Hoag and Ted Gibson of the Demographic Research Unit, California Department of Finance, Sacramento for drivers' license change data.

6 SUB-URBAN AMERICA

While the standard international reference works classify the U.S. as a heavily-urbanized society, its urbs tend to look more like other countries' suburbs – and even its cities are more lightly populated than most others in the world (**4 Elbow Room**). Although suburbia is home to almost half of all Americans, there is no generally agreed definition of the term. The main map shows the "suburban" share of state populations but the data used is merely approximated through the category "metropolitan outside central cities." Indeed definitions are such a problem that even the smaller map, showing central city shares of population, must be interpreted with caution. Arizona may have a large share of its population living in central cities, but Phoenix looks more like a suburb than like Tokyo, Amsterdam, or New York City.

The U.S. government divides the country into metropolitan and non-metropolitan areas. The Office of Management and Budget is responsible for these classifications (though they are based on Census Bureau data). In their view, a metropolitan area is "a core area containing a large population nucleus, together with adjacent communities having a high degree of economic and social integration with that core." To qualify as metropolitan, an area must have one city with 50,000 or more inhabitants, and a total population of 100,000 or more. In essence, the "population nucleus" is the central city and the rest of a metropolitan area its suburbs.

This definition is oversimplified for at least two reasons. For one, the pattern is much more complex in the largest conurbations: New York and Los Angeles, for example, embrace smaller cities and their own satellite suburbs. And for another, suburbs are becoming less and less tied to their central cities. People living in the suburbs can now live, work, and shop for years without setting foot in what government statisticians persist in calling their central city.

The graphic along the bottom of the map shows the huge increase in shopping mall space since the 1960s. American shopping centers are the new Main Streets. The symbols on the main map, highlighting 46 areas, show the high share of office space outside central business districts. It requires a lot of gasoline and highways to live like this, but many Americans probably see this auto-centered routine as civilization's highest form.

Ironically, some older suburbs are displaying problems that used to be thought of as strictly urban – congestion, crime, poverty, racial tension, and fiscal stress. Following an approach once recommended by Henry Ford, many corporations and their well-heeled employees are moving beyond the outer suburbs into formerly rural counties that are now sprouting office parks and new housing developments. A study by American Demographics magazine lists fast-growing counties like Douglas (Colorado), Fayette (Georgia), Loudoun (Virginia) and Hamilton (Indiana) as the "power centers of tomorrow." In twenty years, these budding and currently pristine centers will have probably grown creaky, and will have been replaced by new, formerly rural, power centers for 2030.

Sources to the map:

Swasy, Alecia. "America's 20 Hottest White-Collar Addresses." *Wall Street Journal* (8 March 1994): B1; International Society of Shopping Centers, based on materials published and/or researched by *Shopping Center World* magazine, *Monitor* magazine, and the National Research Bureau; U.S. Bureau of the Census. *Supplementary Report: Metropolitan Areas* (30 June 1993) Washington, D.C., 1993.

Acknowledgment:
Cushman & Wakefield, New York City, New York.

Part Two
ECONOMY

Per capita income is, more formally speaking, real gross domestic product (GDP) per person – that is, the value of goods and services produced in the United States in one year, adjusted for inflation, and divided by the population in that year. Most economists treat this as the best way of measuring economic progress over time, or comparing countries at any moment in time. But this tradition has its shortcomings. It says nothing about the distribution of income, for example. Profits and exports are included in GDP, and those may increase or decrease with little general effect on the population. And average personal incomes reveal nothing about how income is distributed. Real per capita GDP increased by 31% between 1975 and 1992 – but the incomes of the poorest fifth of households increased less than 1%, while the middle fifth's rose 5% and the richest fifth's 28%.

Still, the course of real per capita GDP does provide some measure of economic performance. During the 1960s, a Golden Age of the American economy, it rose an average of 2.5% a year; during the 1970s, the Brass Age, it fell back to 1.7% a year. Despite the hype about the recovery of the U.S. economy during the 1980s per capita income continued to rise at a rate of 1.7% a year. In the slumpish years of 1990-93, per capita GDP rose only 0.4% a year, an index of just how weak that period was.

Sources:
U.S. Bureau of Economic Analysis. "National Income and Product Accounts." Electronic versions from the Economic Bulletin Board, updated with figures from the *Survey of Current Business*, December 1993.

7 MANUFACTURING

Reports to the contrary, manufacturing in America is not dead. Despite the erosion of U.S. firms' positions in some markets, notably consumer electronics and machine tools, industrial production rose smartly overall throughout the 1980s and early 1990s, a period of so-called deindustrialization. In fact, international comparisons are surprisingly flattering to the U.S.: between 1980 and 1993, the growth in U.S. industrial production, according to the Federal Reserve's index, eclipsed all the Group of Seven (G7) countries but Japan; from 1985 to 1993, the U.S. outscored even Japan. (The G7 consists of Canada, France, Germany, Italy, Japan, the U.K., and the U.S.)

From 1980 to 1993, the Federal Reserve's narrower index of manufacturing production, rose 42%. Over the same 13-year period, employment in manufacturing declined by 12%, or 2.5 million jobs, and real (inflation-adjusted) wages fell by 8%. The U.S. now has the second-smallest share of its workforce in manufacturing of the G7 after Canada, and the third-lowest hourly wage after Britain and Japan. This disparity between wages and employment on one hand and production on the other is often celebrated as a productivity miracle, but its miraculousness depends a great deal on where you are standing.

Behind these averages lie an important wealth of detail. A Census Bureau study of over 50,000 manufacturing plants between 1972 and 1988 shows that in an average year, new jobs equaled 9% of manufacturing employment – but over 10% of all jobs were destroyed, resulting in an annual net decline of over 1%. The rapid pace of "creative destruction" (in economist Joseph Schumpeter's phrase) required that almost 12% of all manufacturing workers either became unemployed or had to find a new job every year.

National averages disguise important regional shifts. The states of the Northeast and Midwest have seen the manufacturing share of their economies decline since the late 1970s, some quite dramatically, while the South and West gained. This means that on balance, union jobs were replaced with nonunion ones, and high-wage with lower wage. Yet even those states where manufacturing's share of their economies gained, there was no boom in manufacturing employment. As the inset map shows, manufacturers also set up operations in Mexico – at first, these were for fairly routine assembly work, but by the early 1990s, they were becoming more sophisticated. It also shows that by this time Canada was suffering a similar fate to the U.S. states of the Northeast and Midwest – as high-wage, unionized plants have been shut and production moved to the business-friendly climes of Texas and Mexico.

In theory, displaced manufacturing workers should have little problem finding new work in the rising service sector. A glance at the government's projections of the fastest-growing occupations through 2005, some of which are shown in the bar chart, tempers this theoretical optimism. At the end of 1993, manufacturing jobs paid an average of $509 a week; as they dwindle they will continue to be replaced by jobs in retail trade, where weekly pay averaged $215; business services, $338; and home health care, $297. This shift out of manufacturing is sometimes compared to the shift out of farming several generations ago – but this time, the shift involves pay cuts rather than pay boosts.

Sources to the map:
International Monetary Fund. *International Financial Statistics: 1993 Yearbook*. Washington, D.C., 1994; International Monetary Fund. *International Financial Statistics: March 1994*. Washington, D.C., 1994; "Mexican Maquiladora Employment." *Twin Plant News* (August 1993); Organisation for Economic Cooperation and Development. *OECD in Figures, 1993* (supplement to the *OECD Observer*, June–July 1993); Silvestri, George T. "Occupational Employment: wide variations in Growth." *Monthly Labor Review*, no.116:11(November 1993): 58–86; Statistics Canada; U.S. Department of Commerce. Economic Bulletin Board. Washington, D.C. ; Yuskavage, Robert E. "Gross Product by Industry, 1988-91." *Survey of Current Business*, no. 73:11 (November 1993): 33–44.

Acknowledgment:
Mike Harper of the U.S.Bureau of Labor Statistics, Washington, D.C. for state labor force data.

8 FARMING

Thanks to technology, natural endowments, and generous public supports, American farmers are among the most productive on earth. They produce roughly half the world's corn and soybeans, a fifth of its cotton, and a sixth of its meat. And they do all this with remarkably few hands – less than 2% of the U.S. population, and 0.1% of world population.

While the share of the U.S. population living on farms has declined dramatically, from 44% in 1880 to 15% as recently as 1950 to 1.9% in 1991 – the land area devoted to farming – 43% – has changed little over the same period. That means that output per farmworker and per acre of cropland have both increased enormously. For farmers such gains do not come without a price. The proportion of large-scale farms has increased, and all farmers are under pressure to invest in more and more machinery. Yet as they achieve greater productivity they develop a tendency towards chronic oversupply – bringing downward pressures on raw food prices. Between 1973 and 1993, the prices paid by farmers for equipment and materials rose 176%, while the prices received for their crops grew by only 45%. Government subsidies paid to farmers – which, it is often argued, disproportionally benefit larger operators – make up some of the difference, but the economic pressures on the tillers of the land cannot be blunted completely. It is not only the lure of the city that drives people off U.S. farms.

Federal farm subsidies, which amounted to nearly $18 billion in 1993, are not the only way the government supports the farm sector. Large-scale farming in the western half of the country would be nearly impossible without the vast water projects that cross the landscape; though much of the water infrastructure was built decades ago, over $2 billion of federal money was spent on such projects in 1993 alone. And another $3 billion was spent on agricultural research and extension projects. The money may be well spent, but they belie the old image of the self-reliant farmer.

Family farms continue to dominate U.S. agriculture. Corporations own only 12% of U.S. farmland – but produce 26% of the value of output, making them over twice as productive as family-owned farms. Despite some hysteria in the mid-1980s about foreign takeover of U.S. cropland, less than 2% is actually owned by foreigners, and most of that is forest land. Individual owners are overwhelmingly white (99%) and male (96%), though many other family members of both sexes are pressed into service and their hired hands are disproportionally Hispanic (28% of the total). Many of these hired hands are migrants, who move about the country with the seasons, living and working under the worst circumstances – sleeping in crowded shacks, working without any protection from vile agricultrural chemicals, and paid a pittance for their labor.

At least the debt crisis of the early- and mid-1980s is over. In fact, by one measure, debt as a percentage of income, farmers are in better financial shape than they have been since the 1960s. That does not mean farmers are prospering; the average farming income for the self-employed farm family was over 13% below the average for families headed by nonfarm wage and salary workers in 1992.

Sources to the map:
U.S. Bureau of the Census.*Statistical Abstract of the United States: 1993*. Washington, D.C., 1993. U.S. Department of Commerce. Economic Bulletin Board. Washington, D.C.; Board of Governors of the Federal Reserve System. *Balance Sheets for the U.S. Economy, 1945–92* (June 1993 edition) Washington; D.C., 1993; U.S. Office of Management and Budget.*Budget of the United States Government, Fiscal Year 1995*. Washington, D.C., 1994.

9 FINANCE

In 1991, output of the so-called FIRE sector – finance, insurance, and real estate (excluding construction) – surpassed that of manufacturing. Since the FIRE workforce was only 36% as large, that means that the FIRE worker was roughly three times as productive as the manufacturing worker.

What, after all, do financiers and landlords produce? It is not hard to conceptualize the activity of manufacturing: workers take parts and raw materials and put together finished products, which are then sold for more than their costs of production. That concept translates easily into the national income accounts: value-added, or gross product, equals income from sales less the costs of purchased inputs. That value-added is then divided between workers and owners in the form of wages and profits. But with FIRE, things are less simple; there are no raw materials and there is no tangible finished product.

To circumvent that problem, the national income accountants assume that the value of FIRE's product is simply equal to the costs of providing it – salaries, profits, rent and interest paid, computers, and the like. (This helps explain the bar chart which shows that FIRE output and employment march in virtual lockstep – unlike manufacturing and farming, where technical progress makes it possible to produce more with less.) From another perspective, FIRE's product is equal to what it can charge its customers (since sales on one side equals costs plus profits on the other). While this statistical compromise makes accounting sense, it fails in any intuitive sense to answer the question – what does finance produce?

In economic theory, the financial sector collects society's savings and allocates them to their most productive (defined as most profitable) uses. Even assuming, generously, that is what financiers, realtors, and developers do, it must be noted that they take a very large cut in the process. In 1991, for example, the gross product of the FIRE sector was $1,039 billion a year when gross private investment totaled $737 million. In other words, FIRE's "product" was 41% larger than all national investment. Salaries ($252 billion) and profits ($76 billion) alone were equal to 45% of gross investment.

FIRE pays well. The sector's elite, those employed by security and commodity brokers, earn the highest salary by far of any of the 73 sectors for which the Bureau of Economic Analysis publishes estimates – three times the average of all private sector workers. And workers in finance are the richest group in the Federal Reserve's household financial surveys. FIRE produces wealth for financiers.

Sources to the map:
Ruggles, Richard and Nancy D. Ruggles. "Integrated Economic Accounts for the United States, 1947–80." *Survey of Current Business*, no. 62:5 (May 1982): 1–53; U.S. Bureau of Economic Analysis. "Annual Revision of the National Income and Product Accounts."*Survey of Current Business*, no.73:8 (August 1993):9–51. U.S. Bureau of Labor Statistics. *Employment and Earnings* (January 1993); U.S. Department of Commerce. Economic Bulletin Board. Washington, D.C.; Yuskavage, Robert E. "Gross Product by Industry, 1988–91."*Survey of Current Business*, no.73:11 (November 1993): 33–44.

10 TRADE ROUTES

As recently as the 1960s, international trade accounted for relatively little of the overall U.S. economy. Imports and exports each equaled 5% or less of gross domestic product (GDP). Starting in the late 1960s, however, both measures began a steady upward climb into the low double digits.

Still, a country that was once highly self-reliant has not yet fully adjusted to this new worldliness, and the U.S. economy is still not as global as that of most other rich countries. In 1991, exports were 11% of U.S. GDP, a little ahead of Japan's 10%. (Of course, the U.S. imports more than it exports, unlike Japan, which exports more than it imports.) Most European countries are far more trade-involved than the U.S.: U.K. exports in 1991 were 24% of GDP; France's, 23%; and Germany's 34%.

A few years ago, it was chic to say that the U.S. was becoming Third Worldified – deep in debt to foreign creditors, and with a trade picture more appropriate to a poor country than a rich one (that is, exporting agricultural products and importing manufactured goods). This caricature is wrong. The U.S. does import a high quantity of manufactured goods, but it also exports plenty as well. In 1992, food and beverages accounted for only 9% of U.S. exports. The biggest export items were capital goods like computers, airplanes, and bulldozers (39% of the total), and industrial supplies, like chemicals (24%).

So why does the U.S. still run a large trade deficit? Oil, cars, and consumer electronics are among the most important factors. Once nearly self-sufficient in energy, the U.S. is now a major oil importer; once world leaders in motor vehicles and gadgetry, U.S. producers have lost considerable ground to foreign, mainly Japanese, firms. While auto production of the Big Three manufacturers (General Motors, Chrysler, Ford) is no longer sliding downwards, in the early 1990s, U.S. producers remained weak in consumer electronics.

The geographical pattern of U.S. trade bears a great resemblance to the investment patterns shown in **11 The Search for Profit.** Its major trading partners are mainly part of the First World – Canada, Western Europe, and Japan – and a handful of "newly-industrializing" countries in Asia and Latin America. This is no accident. Trade increasingly follows the channels laid down by the investments of multinational corporations, who do most of the world's cross-border business. National investment patterns reflect this. Just over half of all U.S. trade involves multinational corporations. Of that, a third, or a sixth of all U.S. trade, consists of transfers within these multinationals' global production networks – a shipment of microprocessors, say, from IBM U.S. to IBM Germany, or of auto components from Ford U.S. to Ford Mexico. Due to the multinational corporation, trade and investment have become inseparable.

Sources to the map:
U.S. Bureau of the Census. Cendata computer database, through Compuserve Information Service, Columbus, Ohio; U.S. Department of Commerce. Bureau of Economic Analysis. *National Income and Product Accounts of the United States: Volume 2, 1959-88.* Washington, D.C.

11 THE SEARCH FOR PROFIT

It is now a commonplace that economies are globalizing, and that the world has become one big single market, but the patterns of that integration still require scrutiny. Probably the best model of that process is offered in a series of World Investment Reports issued by the U.N. Programme on Transnational Corporations since 1993, part of the U.N. Conference on Trade and Development (UNCTAD).

Their theory is that international trade and investment flows are dominated by several hundred transnational or multinational corporations (the terms are synonymous) based in what it calls The Triad: the U.S., Western Europe, and Japan. Multinational corporations operate globally, but set up production and distribution networks in all three poles of the Triad, as well as a handful of Third World countries, mainly those near their home bases. These groupings are detailed in the flag graphic on page 34. U.S.-based multinationals, for example, typically have extensive operations in Europe and Japan, but concentrate most of their Third World investments on Latin America, especially Mexico. European multinationals operate extensively in the U.S., less so in Japan, and use eastern and southern Europe the way U.S. firms use Mexico – as low-wage, loosely regulated production sites. The Programme on Transnational Corporations estimates that roughly a third of the world's private sector productive assets are under the control of multinationals pursuing such a strategy of globally integrated production.

This model contradicts two popular misconceptions – one, that the world is breaking into three hostile blocs, and two, that most foreign investment flows are going to the Third World. In fact, 70–80% of foreign direct investment flows between First World countries, with most of the remainder accounted for by fewer than a dozen "newly-industrializing" countries like Brazil, Mexico, China, Indonesia, and Singapore. Africa, Southern and Western Asia, and the small island countries of the Caribbean and the Pacific are almost completely out of this picture.

U.S. companies were at the forefront of multinationalization, but European and Japanese companies have been catching up. That means that from the American point of view, investment no longer flows in just one direction – outward. One in 20 U.S. workers is now employed by a foreign firm, and almost one in eight manufacturing workers. But since European and Japanese firms are relatively recent arrivals in the U.S., their operations are far less profitable than well-established U.S. operations are abroad; these foreign-owned companies have been hampered not only by start-up costs, but also by the inflated prices they paid during the Roaring Eighties. By comparison U.S. firms paid more reasonable prices in the 1960s and 1970s when they were going through the same process.

Sources to the map:
U.S. Bureau of Economic Analysis. Economic Bulletin Board: statistical release BEA-93-42 (22 September 1993) Washington, D.C.; U.S.Bureau of Economic Analysis.*Survey of Current Business* (July 1993) Washington, D.C.; U.N. Conference on Trade and Development. Programme on Transnational Corporations.*World Investment Report 1993: Transnational Corporations and Integrated International Production* (ST/CTC/156) New York: United Nations, 1993; U.N. Department of Economic and Social Development.*World Investment Report 1992: Transnational Corporations as Engines of Growth* (ST/CTC/130) New York: United Nations, 1992.

12 WINNERS AND LOSERS

The dynamism of the American economy cannot be denied. Firms grow and shrink, are born and die, with headspinning speed. Similar things happen to regions. The recession of the early 1980s savaged the industrial and farming Midwest, but left the coasts largely untouched; the heartland barely recovered in the mid-1980s, but Texas collapsed along with oil prices, and the Northeast and California soared, thanks to the booms in finance, real estate, the media, and the law. But when the postindustrial boom fell apart in the late 1980s, the Midwest was largely unscathed, and even perked up a bit on a recovery in manufacturing at the turn of the decade. The South has also been enjoying a regional boom, thanks to new investments by both U.S. and foreign manufacturers, and the Mountain states and the Pacific Northwest have benefited from the exodus of people and capital from southern California. Yet even as the national economy took off in 1992 and 1993, New York as well as California, the capitals of the Roaring Eighties, remained mired in local slumps.

Longer term patterns can be read from the inset map in which up and down arrows trace the movement of the headquarters of Fortune 500 companies. Firms swarmed out of their glass-and-steel towers in New York City beginning in the 1960s in favor of campus-like suburban headquarters in New Jersey and Connecticut; more recently, some of the early suburban movers have left the Northeast for places like Virginia and Texas. As old-line Rustbelt firms with headquarters in Ohio and Pennsylvania failed, fell off the top 500, or were acquired, new firms in new industries like electronics and aerospace rose in California. And all was not death and destruction in the Midwest; mass production may have seen better days, but more highly specialized steel and chemical producers moved in.

Hints of the promising sectors of the mid-1990s can be found in *Business Week's* 1993 list of 250 hot growth companies. Of the top 50 companies on this list, almost a quarter are in computers and electronics, and a fifth are in health care. Finance, the hot area of the 1980s, has dropped away. And company success can be fleeting: Merry-Go-Round, a clothing retailer that was no. 41 on the *Business Week* list, filed for bankruptcy in early 1994.

Sources to the map:
Dun & Bradstreet Corporation. Press releases on business failures and new incorporations. New York, various dates; "The Forbes 400" *Forbes* (18 October 1993): 110-31; "The Fortune 500" *Fortune* (19 April 1993): 174-288; "250 Companies on the Move." *Business Week*. Special issue on "Enterprise" (no date, 1993).

13 SHADES OF GREEN

A state could have clean air and toxic water – so it is hard to imagine a single indicator that could convey environmental quality. Fortunately, the Institute for Southern Studies (Raleigh, N.C.) has taken a close look at the ecological health of every state, and produced a composite "green index." Researchers drew up 179 measures of environmental quality for a single "green conditions" index, and 77 measures of environmental policy to make a "green policies" index, ranking states according to their scores. They then combined the two sub-indexes to create a composite "green index."

Since we had to choose a single measure, the green conditions index is shown here. This reflects the current state of the physical environment that people must live in and is not colored by commitments to policies that may never be implemented. But, according to the Institute, there are some interesting disparities between conditions and policies. Some mountain states scored far higher on conditions than policies; ironically, many leading anti-environmental politicians hail from the most pristine states in the country. Meanwhile some of the old industrial states of the Northeast and Midwest exhibit just the opposite pattern – having inherited a despoiled nature from their industrial pasts, they are showing some commitment to cleaning things up.

Components of the green conditions index include measures of air pollution; water pollution; energy use and production; transportation efficiency; solid, toxic and hazardous waste; community and workplace health; agricultural pollution; the health of forest and fish life; and recreational amenities.

Arkansas, the state that President Clinton governed for over a decade, scored badly on both conditions (48th) and policies (50th). Clinton's early federal budgets have squeezed environmental enforcement, energy research, and public transit assistance – despite the environmental interests of the Vice President.

Evidence on global warming and ozone depletion may not persuade skeptics and corporate lobbyists, who may have to be convinced the hard way, when crops burn and skin cancers become endemic. But convincing evidence that air pollution kills people comes from Douglas W. Dockery and his colleagues at the Harvard School of Public Health. Their study of particulate air pollution (tiny airborne particles, including soot, smoke, and dust emitted by cars, factories, power plants, and construction sites) in six U.S. cities shows clearly that the higher the filth level, the higher the death rate.

The U.S. preserves a greater proportion of its land in national parks and other museums of nature than most other countries – but extravagant tastes in cars and packaging, and an acceptance of urban and suburban sprawl, means that Americans are big energy consumers who pump out high levels of greenhouse gases, and create Mount Everests of garbage. Ironically, the view at the Grand Canyon is increasingly blurred by smog.

Sources to the map:
Dockery, Douglas W. et al. "An Association Between Air Pollution and Mortality in Six U.S. Cities." *New England Journal of Medicine*, no. 329 (9 December 1993): 1753–1759; Organisation for Economic Cooperation and Development. *Environmental Indicators*. Paris: O.E.C.D., 1991; Whitelegg, John. "Dirty from Cradle to Grave." *The Guardian* (17 June 1993); U.S. Environmental Protection Agency. *National Air Quality and Emissions Trends Report, 1992.* Research Triangle Park, NC, 1993.

Acknowledgments:
Bob Hall and Mary Lee Kerr of the Institute for Southern Studies, Raleigh, NC for compiling the Green Index and for permission to reproduce it.

14 LABOR

One generalization that can safely be made about working life in the U.S. – and the rest of the industrial world – at the end of the 20th century, is that uncertainty is on the rise. Long gone are the days when a fresh high school graduate could go down to the factory and pick up a decent job, or a college graduate could get an even more decent white-collar job, both having the reasonable prospect of staying with their employers for the rest of their working lives – or moving on to an even better job, if ambition or restlessness called. This scenario was always more open to the white and male than the non-white and female, but for a long time it has been a common enough pattern.

This has now all but changed. In the late 1970s, blue collar manufacturing jobs began to disappear in droves, as firms began automating, outsourcing, moving offshore, and replacing permanent, full-time workers with temporary and part-time ones. By the late 1980s, similar disruptions began to hit previously shielded sectors and occupations – the service industries, middle management, and even the elite professions. Well before the 1990–91 recession began, announcements of mass layoffs by Fortune 500 firms became a staple of the business news, and continue well after its end.

All the institutions that traditionally acted as buffers between workers and the unsentimental mechanisms of the labor market have eroded – whether formal, like unions and collective bargaining contracts, or informal, like the implied lifetime job contract between large firms and their white collar workforce. In the early 1950s, almost a third of the workforce was unionized; now it is less than a sixth – with just three states (California, New York, and Illinois) accounting for almost a third of union membership. If this trend were to continue, unions could disappear entirely in a couple of decades. And workers not only cycle in and out of jobs, they even change their occupations.

Economists generally applaud this de-buffering as the elimination of "rigidities" that hamper the efficient functioning of the marketplace; workers with 30-year mortgages and orthodontal bills view it quite differently. In Western Europe, these buffers, along with a far more generous welfare state, have also been under heavy attack since the 1980s but they are still much more protective than in the U.S. – which is probably why workers in a dozen European countries have higher hourly wage rates than Americans.

It is sometimes said that trade unions benefit mainly white men, and a privileged subset of white men at that. Union leaders may show an appalling tendency towards racial and sexual callousness, but our average wage graphic shows that unions significantly boost the wages of women and nonwhites as well. Unionized white women and unionized black and Hispanic men all have higher weekly wages than nonunion white men, with unionized black women not far behind. Organizations can protect the discriminated-against, while the otherwise privileged have an easier time fending for themselves.

Sources to the map:
Employment and Earnings (January 1993); Hirsch, Barry and David Macpherson. "Union Membership and Coverage Files from the Current Population Surveys: Note." *Industrial and Labor Relations Review* (April 1993); Troy, Leo and Neil Sheflin. *U.S. Union Sourcebook.* West Orange, NJ: IRDIS, 1985. U.S. Bureau of Labor Statistics. *International Comparisons of Hourly Compensation Costs for Production Workers in Manufacturing, 1992.* Washington, D.C., 1993.

Acknowledgment:
Barry Hirsch for sharing his data on state unionization rates. This data used to be published by the Bureau of Labor Statistics until the practice was suspended early in the Reagan era. The information is still collected, however, and Hirsch and Macpherson (see above) analyze it annually.

15 WOMEN WORKING

Though the trend seems to have slowed a little in the early 1990s, the steady rise in the share of women working for pay has been one of the most important social developments in modern history. In 1948, less than a third of all women worked for pay (and "for pay" is an important qualification, since they have always worked without pay in the household.) Now, almost 60% are at work or actively looking for work. At the same time, the share of men working or looking for work – the labor force participation rate – has fallen from 87% in 1948 to 76% in 1993.

The occupational gender gap persists, but it is getting narrower. The wages graphic shows how women's earnings have risen as a percentage of men's for year-round, full-time workers between 1980 and 1992. For all workers the gap has also narrowed: from 47% of men's in 1980 to 62% in 1992. The occupations graphic also shows that women are entering elite professions in much larger numbers.

The news is not all good. Where earnings are concerned, recent gains by women have as much been the result of losses by men. Men's real (inflation-adjusted) earnings have fallen steadily over the last 20 years, while those for women have risen steadily. Despite the narrowing wage gap, female professionals and executives still earn 30 percent less than their male counterparts. And despite women's penetration of upscale jobs, they remain few and far between in skilled, high-paying blue-collar trades like construction, carpentry, and plumbing. Nor have traditionally "female" jobs become much more mixed. All but 1% of secretaries are female, and all but 6% of nurses – virtually unchanged from 1972. At the top, gender integration is becoming the norm, but further down the status ladder, occupational segregation persists.

Women's increasing involvement in paid work has produced little change in the amount of their unpaid labor. Housekeeping and child care remain largely their responsibility and since full-time motherhood is something only affluent families can afford, arranging child care is one of the many challenges facing working women. According to the statistics, arrangements are often spotty and informal, with mothers' workweeks exceeding child care availability by an average of seven hours.

Only 8% of all employees of large- and mid-sized business are eligible for child care benefits at work, and 1% of small business employees. About 40% of all families with working mothers have to pay for child care, at an average of 7% of their total income. Single mothers who pay for child care devote over 10% of their income for this, while the working poor spend over 20%. Child care is expensive, but not because the minders of children are highly paid: in 1993, they earned an average of $6.69 an hour, 4% less than parking lot attendants, who earned $6.95.

Sources to the map:
Employment and Earnings (January 1990, January 1991, January 1993, October 1993, and November 1993); Fuller, Bruce and Xiaoyan Liang. *The Unfair Search for Child Care.* Cambridge, MA: Harvard University School of Education, 1993; O'Connell, Martin and Amara Bachu. "Who's Minding the Kids?: Child Care Arrangements." *Household Economic Studies*, P70-30 (August 1992) Washington, D.C.: U.S. Bureau of the Census, 1992; U.S. Bureau of the Census.*Statistical Abstract of the United States:1993.* Washington, D.C., 1993; U.S. Bureau of the Census. "Money Income of Households, Families, and Persons in the United States: 1992." *Current Population Reports*, no. 60-184 (September 1993) Washington, D.C., 1993; U.S. Bureau of Labor Statistics."Earnings Differences Between Women and Men." *Facts on Working Women*, no. 90-93 (October 1990) Washington, D.C., 1990; U.S. Bureau of Labor Statistics. *Handbook of Labor Statistics.* Washington, D.C., 1989; U.S. Bureau of Labor Statistics.*Geographical Profile of Employment and Unemployment* (various issues) Washington, D.C.

16 PERSONAL INCOME

While average incomes are highest in the Northeast, these averages are complicated by two factors – the presence of some the very rich who skew the figures upwards, and a higher cost of living. Figures simply do not exist that would compensate for differences in living costs, so the reported averages have to be taken at face value. But, thanks to Citizens for Tax Justice, there are figures available on income distribution by state.

In-state inequality, it seems, comes in two major forms. The first kind is that seen in rich states, like New York (home to Wall Street) and California (home to Hollywood and Silicon Valley). Of course, both states also have large minority populations, and non-whites are much poorer than whites. The other kind is that seen in the southern and mountain states, where few are rich, but many are poor. Both kinds of inequality may be present in Florida and Texas. The figures of Citizens for Tax Justice show that the Midwest is the most egalitarian region in the country, where average incomes may be middling by national standards, but extremes of wealth and poverty are relatively infrequent.

According to estimates by the Congressional Budget Office, when these statistical snapshots were taken in the early 1990s, the richest 1% of the population claimed over 12% of all personal income after taxes, nearly three times as much as the poorest 20%, and almost as much as the entire bottom 40% of the income distribution. The richest fifth – containing everyone from the upper-middle-class to the super-rich – pulled down just under half of all American incomes. Inequality on this level has not been seen in the U.S. since the 1920s, and nowhere else in the First World is it so extreme.

Incomes given in the sex and ethnic comparisons refer to income from all sources – everything from investments to alimony payments – unlike those shown in **14 Labor** and **15 Women Working**, which refer only to income from employment.

The Gini index may be a touch arcane but it is the most effective known means of expressing a difficult concept. The Gini, though intuitively meaningless in itself, compares income distribution across countries, or in a single country across time. The higher the figure, the more unequal the distribution. Incomes measured here are cash incomes after taxes and transfer payments (pension benefits, unemployment and welfare benefits, etc.).

Sources to the map:
Citizens for Tax Justice. *A Far Cry From Fair: CTJ's Guide to State Tax Reform.* Washington, D.C., 1991; U.S. Bureau of Economic Analysis. *Total Personal Income by State, 1987-92.* Statistical release (27 April 1993).

Acknowledgments:
John Coder of the U.S. Bureau of the Census for computing the international Gini indexes; Citizens for Tax Justice for the first state-by-state analysis of income distribution, and for permission to reproduce the figures.

17 TAXES

New York has a reputation as a high-tax state, and Texas as a low-tax one. A look at the share of personal income claimed by state and local governments in each jurisdiction confirms these perceptions: New York's bite, relative to state personal income, is almost 40% higher than that of Texas. But a closer look shows that for the poor, Texas cannot be considered a low-tax regime: in 1991, the poorest fifth of Texans paid over 17% of their income to state and local taxpersons, compared with 14% in New York. But at the top, it was another story: the richest 1% of Texans paid just over 3% of their income in state and local taxes, while upper-crust New Yorkers paid 11.3%. The picture was similar in other supposedly low-tax states outside the Northeast.

When the balance of payments with Washington is added in, the regional picture becomes even more interesting. Sunbelt states whose politicians have made careers of denouncing Washington nonetheless have a good deal going – they get more back in federal spending than they pay in federal taxes, thanks to largesse like weapons contracts, water and highway projects, and farm subsidies. These inflows are funded by outflows from the Northeast, where federal programs are generally (and perhaps strangely) more popular.

Six states – Florida, Nevada, South Dakota, Tennessee, and Washington, as well as Texas – all taxed their poorest 20% at a rate more than four times as high as their richest 1% in 1991. Only six states – Delaware, Hawaii, Maryland, Minnesota, Oregon, and Vermont – squeezed their poor less tightly than their rich. For the middle fifth, the picture was a little brighter, but not much; they were taxed less heavily than the poor, but nonetheless more heavily than the rich in all but four states – California, Delaware, Maine, and Vermont. Yet for all the tax rebellions of the last 20 years, the deeply regressive nature of most state tax systems is hardly mentioned in public.

Similar things can be said on an international scale. The U.S. has a reputation as a low-tax country – on average. In 1991, all taxes paid accounted for 30% of gross domestic product (GDP) in the U.S., compared with 41% in the European Union. But the tax bite, measured as a percentage of gross pay, on the average married American worker with two children was deeper than in many European countries and was almost as deep as Germany's. And for their taxes, Europeans get free or cheap education, health insurance, public transit, and child care.

While personal income is used as the denominator in these tax burden measures, the taxes come from businesses as well as individuals. Personal income is used rather than gross state product (GSP) because personal income measures are more timely and probably more accurate than GSP figures.

Sources to the map:
Citizens for Tax Justice. *A Far Cry From Fair.* CTJ's Guide to State Tax Reform. Washington, D.C., 1991; Office of Senator Daniel Patrick Moynihan, in association with the Taubman Center for State and Local Government. John F. Kennedy School of Government, Harvard University. *Baumol's Disease.* New York State and the Federal Fisc, no. XVII (29 July 1993): 26-27; Organisation for Economic Cooperation and Development. *OECD in Figures, 1993.* (supplement to the *OECD Observer,* June–July 1993); U.S. Bureau of the Census.Government Finances: 1989–90 (GF/90-5, December 1991) Washington, D.C.,

1991; U.S. General Accounting Office. *State and Local Finances: Some Jurisdictions Confronted by Short- and Long-Term Problems* (GAO/HRD-94-1, October 1993) Washington, D.C., 1993.

Acknowledgments:
The Citizens for Tax Justice for sharing the first detailed analysis of state tax systems.

18 THE PROMISED LAND

Poverty in America is a sensitive subject and public discussion rarely gets further than clichés. From listening to talk radio one would get the impression that U.S. poverty is mainly an affair of single, "minority" teenage mothers living in big cities, who suffer from a heritable predilection for being on welfare.

Though the poverty rate for urban black and Hispanic single-mother families is over 50%, they constitute a seventh (14%) of the American poor. White suburbanites account for almost twice as many of the poor (24%). And studies of what social scientists call the "intergenerational transmission of welfare dependency" do not support popular "like mother, like daughter" stereotypes. About one in five daughters of "highly welfare dependent" mothers themselves became highly welfare dependent, with the rest showing only light welfare use or none at all. Most single mothers began their spells on welfare because of a divorce or a husband's death. In recent years, there has been a sharp growth in the number of single mothers who were never married. But in the words of a 1992 General Accounting Office report, "The new growth in never-married mothers...differed from the stereotype: They were not unemployed teenaged dropouts but rather working women aged 25 to 44 who had completed high school."

This is not to deny the existence of a cohort of urban teenage mothers with few prospects. But within American society there are many other groups of poor people: urban, suburban, and rural; working and unemployed; abled and disabled; young and old; white, black, Hispanic, and every other ethnic group.

When income classes are defined relative to national averages, the U.S. has the highest number of poor and the smallest middle-class of a dozen rich countries. This is shown by the work of the Luxembourg Income Study, an international effort to study income distribution around the world. If poverty is defined as having an income less than half the national median (a common scholarly definition of poverty), if near-poverty is defined as having an income between 50% and 62.5% of the median, and if being middle-class is defined as having 62.5% and 150% of the median, then almost a quarter of the U.S. population is poor or near-poor, and less than half is middle-class. In Sweden, by these definitions, nearly three-quarters of the population is middle-classs and only one-eighth are poor. Germany and the Netherlands show slightly larger poor and near-poor populations, and somewhat smaller middle- classes.

Definitions of poverty are politically explosive and, as this graphic shows, widely varying. In the U.S., the official definition is based on 1950s research, which showed the average family spent a third of its income on food; therefore, government statisticians reasoned, a poverty income was three times what they thought the minimum food budget should be. The poverty line was thus fixed in 1963, and has simply been adjusted for inflation ever since – with no allowance made for all the changes of the last 30 years, notably the sharp rise in the cost of housing, medical care, and child care. Work by Patricia Ruggles, of the Urban Institute in Washington D.C., has shown that a similar calculation today, based on a modern market basket, would yield a poverty rate nearly twice as high as the official rate.

Other definitions have been formulated which also produce rather different results from the official figures. Adam Smith observed that poverty is relative, being defined by the lack of those necessities that "the custom of the country renders it indecent for creditable people, even of the lowest order, to be without." Thus poverty in Mexico is different from poverty in the U.S., and poverty in 1993 is different from 1963. The half-the-median formula is an approach based on this thinking. By this measure, Jack McNeil of the U.S. Census Bureau has estimated that the 1991 poverty rate was over 22 percent.

Conservatives, however, have long objected to both the official measure and relative measures. They argue that today's poor enjoy a standard of living beyond Marie Antoinette's, with T.V., Big Macs, and a far longer life expectancy. They also argue that the official measure, along with others confined to cash income, ignores the value of noncash benefits, like Food Stamps, rent subsidies, and Medicaid, and also ignores the value of "housing services" consumed by poor people who own the houses they live in. ("Consumption of housing services" is how economists describe the pleasures of sleeping in your bedroom or eating in your dining room.) For the last several years, the Census Bureau, under this conservative pressure, has been publishing alternative measures of poverty that redefine penury according to 14 experimental measures. When government benefits are included – noncash benefits and owner-occupied housing, as in the fifth definition shown – the poverty rate in 1992 comes down from 14.5% to 10.4%. But this masks the fact that the poor cannot fend for themselves.

Sources to the map:
Coder, John. Unpublished relative income figures from the Luxembourg Income Study database. Washington, D.C.: U.S. Bureau of the Census; Ruggles, Patricia. Statement before the Select Committee on Hunger. U.S. House of Representatives (4 October 1990); U.S. Bureau of the Census. "Measuring the Effect of Benefits and Taxes on Income and Poverty: 1992." *Current Population Reports*, Series P-60, no. 186RD. Washington, D.C., 1992; U. S. Bureau of the Census. "Poverty in the United States: 1992." *Current Population Reports*, Series P-60, no. 185. Washington, D.C., 1992; U.S. Bureau of the Census. "Trends in Relative Income: 1964 to 1989." *Current Population Reports*, Series P-60, no. 177. Washington, D.C., 1991; U.S. General Accounting Office. *Poverty Trends, 1980–88: Changes in Family Composition and Income Sources Among the Poor* (GAO/PEMD-92-34, September 1992) Washington, D.C., 1992; U.S. House of Representatives. Committee on Ways and Means. "Intergenerational Welfare Receipt." In 1992 *Green Book*: 689-92. Washington, D.C.: U.S. Government Printing Office, 1992.

Acknowledgments:
John Coder and Jack McNeil of the U.S. Bureau of the Census for computing the international poverty and income figures, and for sharing unpublished 1991 data on relative incomes, respectively.

Part Three
SOCIETY

Composite measures like the Human Development Index (HDI) are extremely useful, but many devils lurk in the details. Showing the major U.S. ethnic groups separately – white, black, and Hispanic – addresses in part one of the shortcomings, the fact that averages by their very nature can conceal great extremes. As the old joke goes, if you ask someone who has one foot in boiling water and the other frozen in ice how they are doing, they could answer, "On average, not bad."

But even more diabolical complexities lurk behind the construction of the composite index. How do you weight the components? In the HDI's case, are income, literacy, years of schooling, and life expectancy all of equal importance? And how do you define the components? Does a dollar of income above a certain minimum count as much as a dollar below it? And what about income distribution? (If the share of income going to the poor were included in the HDI, the U.S. ranking would fall several notches, and it would fall several more if the HDI were adjusted for gender disparities.) Is literacy the ability to write one's name, or to understand Shakespeare? (For more on literacy and the HDI see **21 Literacy and Learning**.) How much do years of schooling matter if the textbooks are obsolete and the teachers poorly trained? And is there a hidden agenda behind the very invention of the HDI? Is it, as some sources within the U.N. have suggested, an attempt to divert attention from global income inequality in the guise of a more humane concern for non-economic values?

Source:
United Nations Development Program. *Human Development Report 1993*. New York: Oxford University Press, 1993.

19 A START IN LIFE

For those who believe that birth rates are a measure of social vigor, the picture shown in the main map will be no surprise: the older states of the Northeast show the lowest birth rates, and the younger ones in the South and West, the highest. Despite its climate, Alaska seems to have more in common with the sunbelt than the snowbelt.

American infants do not necessarily have an easy time of it. Infant mortality rates – deaths within the first year of life – are the highest in the First World; Washington, D.C.'s rate of 21 deaths per 1,000 live births is higher than that of Hungary and not much below the rate in Argentina. Low birthweight is the biggest single determinant of survival and an important predictor of general health. The share of infants born with dangerously low weight in D.C. is about the same as in Mexico. Why is this? Lack of access to medical care during pregnancy, usually a function of poverty, is probably an important factor. In fact, the World Bank uses infant mortality rates (along with primary school enrollment) as a measure of poverty in the Third World, where social statistics are often spotty and difficult to compare across countries.

As so often, average figures obscure contradictions. Infant mortality figures for U.S. whites are not much higher than in Europe, though they are more than half again as high as in Japan. This confirms the impression (no firm numbers are available) that Japanese poverty rates are among the lowest in the world. But the infant mortality rate for U.S. blacks is over twice the rate for whites and over three times the rate in Japan. Although comparative figures are not shown on the map, similar patterns hold for life expectancy at birth. Both black men and women have a much shorter life expectancy than whites of both sexes, who are among the longest-lived people in the world.

Sources to the map:
Organisation for Economic Cooperation and Development. *OECD in Figures: Statistics on the Member Countries* (supplement to the *OECD Observer*, June–July 1993); U.S. Bureau of the Census. *Statistical Abstract of the United States: 1993.* Washington, D.C., 1993; World Bank. "Implementing the World Bank's Strategy to Reduce Poverty: Progress and Challenges." *World Development Report* (April 1993).

20 FAMILIES

If the family is the fundamental unit of society, American society is undergoing a fundamental restructuring. "Traditional" families break up far more often than they used to, more people – children included – are living in nontraditional households, and many members of unorthodox households are demanding rights and benefits previously available to orthodox ones. Over 3 million opposite-sex couples live together without the blessing of the state, and no one knows how many same-sex ones do.

Marriage rates have remained rather stable over the last 40 years. They fell somewhat between 1950 and 1960, as the post-World War II marriage and baby boom petered out, but rose slightly between 1960 and 1988, as the graphic shows. But during the latter period, the divorce rate doubled. Roughly one in two marriages now ends in divorce – although many people remarry and 40% of all marriages are second or later unions. The increase in divorce means that about two-and-a-half times more children are involved in divorces than in the 1950s. That, plus the increasing share of births outside marriage (3% of the total in 1950, 11% in 1970, and 28% in 1990), means that almost a third of all children do not live with both their parents. For black children, a two-parent household is the exception, not the norm; only 36% live with both their parents, compared with 65% of Hispanic children and 77% of white children.

The regional picture of marriage and divorce does not really conform to standard preconceptions – especially divorce. As the map shows, some of the highest divorce rates can be found in the South and West, professed strongholds of traditional values, while some of the lowest can be found in the "liberal" states of the Northeast and upper Midwest. In New York the divorce rate is 40% of the marriage rate, while the equivalent figure in Arizona is 73%.

The two pie charts show extensive change in the percentages of household types in the U.S. and as the bar chart shows, the U.S. ranks rather highly in the number of births outside marriage. Although not shown on the map, compared with other Western countries, a surprisingly high share of Americans lives in households other than the traditional married-with-children kind. Canada, France, Germany, Japan, and the Netherlands all have a greater share of their populations living in married-with-children households.

None of these figures are recited to urge a return to the old days, or to argue that conventional married-couple households are better than other kinds. They are intended instead to show that national self-image and public policy have not really caught up with the changes in family life. Other Western countries provide child allowances, subsidized day care, and universal health insurance coverage to support not just the traditional but also the non-traditional household.

Sources to the map:
U.N. Development Programme. *Human Development Report 1993*. New York: Oxford University Press, 1993; U.S. Bureau of the Census.*Statistical Abstract of the United States:1993*. Washington, D.C., 1993; U.S. Bureau of the Census. *Historical Statistics of the United States, Colonial Times to 1970*. Washington, D.C.: U.S. Government Printing Office, 1976; U.S. National Center for Health Statistics. *Health, United States, 1992*. Hyattsville, MD: NCHS, 1993.

Acknowledgment:
Sally Clarke of the National Center for Health Statistics for decoding marriage and divorce data.

21 LITERACY AND LEARNING

The U.S. spends a large share of its gross domestic product (GDP) on education (5.7 percent in 1988) on schooling, but the real problem is not funding but quality. The statistics on verbal and mathematical literacy are deeply disturbing.

The quality of literacy is difficult to measure. Of 20 rich industrial countries, eight (Canada and seven European countries) outspend the U.S. when education spending is measured as a share of GDP. But a large share of U.S. spending is devoted to higher education, and the share of the population of school age is relatively high. When these factors are taken into account, U.S. education spending in relation to GDP is much lower than it would appear. A 1990 study, using 1985 data, and adjusted for variations in enrollment, by the Economic Policy Institute, puts the U.S. at 14th out of 16 countries in the share of GDP devoted to primary and secondary education.

Similar comparisons for literacy are virtually impossible. When the U.N. Development Program published its first *Human Development Report* in 1990, the U.S. ranked 18th in the world in overall development, in large part because the government reported that 4 percent of adults were illiterate. Resulting bad press led to an official rethink: Washington quickly told the U.N. that the American illiteracy rate had dropped to 1 percent, which contributed to the nation's rise to 7th in overall development in 1991. Yet in that same year, an inquiry on illiteracy (defined as a fourth-grade reading level or less) made to the U.S. Department of Education yielded a press release estimating illiteracy at 13 percent. Another third of adults were called "functionally illiterate," and another half, "marginally literate" – leaving only 5 percent as fully literate. These figures refer to literacy in English only; 14 percent of all Americans speak a language other than English at home. Even allowing for that, however, the level of officially defined illiteracy remains appallingly high.

Those figures were based on a 1982 survey, which is the source for the state figures shown here. Unfortunately, no more recent state figures are available. More recent national figures are available, and these cover arithmetic and analytical skills as well as reading. They are illustrated in the pie chart. In early 1992, the U.S. Department of Education interviewed 13,600 people for The National Adult Literacy Survey. This study broke down literacy into three parts: prose, document, and quantitative. Prose literacy is the ability to read a passage and answer questions about it; document literacy, the ability to comprehend things like bus schedules, maps, and graphs; and quantitative literacy, the ability to balance a checkbook, or fill out an order form, or compute bank interest. Results on each part of the survey were scored on a scale from 1 (lowest) to 5 (highest). Our pie chart averages the scores on the three parts and combines levels 1 and 2 into low, levels 4 and 5 into high, and calls level 3 medium.

The results, while not easily comparable to the 1982 survey, are hardly less appalling. Those scoring at the lowest levels – almost half the population – could not, on average, write a letter contesting an error made on a credit card bill or decode a bus schedule, tasks typical of level 3 skills. Those scoring at level 3 or below – nearly 80 percent of adults – were unable to summarize newspaper editorials, describe patterns in oil imports shown in a chart, or figure change by adding up the cost of items on a menu. Those scoring at level 4 or below – 97 percent of adults – were unable to draw a graph when confronted with raw numbers, or figure the cost of carpeting a room when given a calculator, the room's dimensions, and the carpet's cost per square foot.

But the literacy-challenged do not necessarily perceive themselves as such. Over two-thirds of the level 1s and nine-tenths of the level 2s thought themselves able to read and write English "well" or "very well."

Sources to the map:
"Definitions and Estimates." *Adult Learning & Literacy Clearinghouse Fact Sheet*, no.4 (October 1987); Rasell, M. Edith and Lawrence Mishel. *Shortchanging Education: How U.S. Spending on Grades K–12 Lags Behind Other Industrial Nations.* Washington, D.C.: Economic Policy Institute, 1990; U.S. Department of Education. *Adult Literacy in America: A First Look at the Results of the National Adult Literacy Survey* (September) Washington, D.C., 1993; U.S. Bureau of the Census.*Statistical Abstract of the United States: 1993.* Washington, D.C., 1993; U.S. Bureau of the Census. *Government Finances: 1989–90,* Series GF/90-5 (December 1991) Washington, D.C. 1991.

22 A MODERN PLAGUE

The prevalence in large coastal cities reflects the demographics of the disease: it started mainly as a disease of gay men and injecting drug users and, despite its spread beyond those original risk groups, remains disproportionally their plague.

When the earliest cases of AIDS were first reported in 1981, the disease was thought to be a medical curiosity, of no great general interest. In the U.S., the first demographic group to be affected was gay men. And in the early days, as Randy Shilts, who died of the disease in early 1994, recounted in his classic history, even gay men were unable to believe there was much of an emergency at first.

For thousands of gay men it was already too late. But they renounced unsafe sex and organized to educate their peers and to confront an indifferent-to-hostile scientific–pharmaceutical complex. Reaganites withheld funding, often arguing that the best prevention was "to just say no." As it became clear that injecting drug users were another group coming down with AIDS in vast numbers, the moralistic approach was reinforced. There was a sense among both the government and mainstream America that somehow people had brought the disease on themselves. The devout were prepared to go further, and see it as God's punishment for sodomy and addiction.

Instead of increasing the use of condoms and allowing the distribution of clean hypodermic needles, officials and pundits talked about abstinence (a fanciful strategy) and continue to do so a decade later. The disease has continued to spread, especially among the poor and nonwhite. The disporportional number of black Americans and Hispanics suffering from AIDS seemed to confirm the opinion of white, heterosexual America that it was a disease of "them," rather than "us." As long ago as 1982, these groups accounted for just under half the men and over three-quarters of women with AIDS. In recent years, rates of infection have been increasing most rapidly in smaller cities and in rural areas.

In 1994, blacks and Hispanics with AIDS are still likely to die more quickly once they get the disease, because of poor underlying health and restricted access to care. As yet, they have been unable to lobby for public health measures or more effective treatment, or develop education programs. Since gay men have changed their behavior remarkably, AIDS is increasingly a disease of injecting drug users and their sexual partners, who often have the vaguest ideas, if any, of how the disease spreads.

Though AIDS is still highly concentrated in large cities, as the map shows, the rate of infection in smaller cities and the countryside is increasing rapidly. AIDS is a new disease, but it has helped revive an old one – tuberculosis. New cases of TB had been declining for decades, and in the mid-1980s it was on the verge of being wiped out. Though some 10–15 million Americans carry the tuberculosis infection, a healthy immune system usually keeps it under control, preventing its spread. But when AIDS reduces the body's defense system and resistance, formerly latent TB becomes the real thing. The social crisis among the poor has hastened the spread of both AIDS and TB. One-fifth of the new TB cases in New York City occurs among the homeless. The shelters and steam tunnels, where the homeless congregate, are ideal breeding sites. Yet despite the problem, the authorities have been slow to react. Funding for research, public health measures, and treatment remains squeezed at every level of government. Many of the most recent TB cases are resistant to standard drug therapies which makes them more costly to treat. Curiously the cost of TB drugs has risen sharply. Between 1986 and 1992, the cost of drugs used to treat a simple case rose from $209 to $353, or 69%, and for a complex, drug-resistant case, from $2,600 to $8,720, or 235%.

Sources to the map:

Buckmire, Ron. The Queer Resources Directory computer database, through the Internet gopher program; Shilts, Randy. *And the Band Played On: Politics, People, and the AIDS Epidemic.* New York: Penguin Books, 1988; U.S. Centers for Disease Control and Prevention. *AIDS Information: Statistical Projections/Trends.* Document no. 320210 (1993); U.S. Centers for Disease Control and Prevention. *HIV/AIDS Prevention.* CDC National AIDS Hotline Training Bulletin, no. 43 (5 April 1993); U.S. Centers for Disease Control and Prevention. *HIV/AIDS Surveillance Report* (March 1991); U.S. Centers for Disease Control and Prevention. *HIV/AIDS Surveillance Report* (July 1993); U.S. Centers for Disease Control and Prevention. *National Action Plan to Combat Multidrug-Resistant Tuberculosis* (April 1992); U.S. Centers for Disease Control and Prevention. *Morbidity and Mortality Weekly Report* (10 September 1993). U.S. Congress. Office of Technology Assessment.*The Continuing Challenge of Tuberculosis*, OTA-H-574 (September 1993) Washington, D.C., 1993; U.S. National Commission on AIDS. *AIDS in Rural America* (1990); U.S. National Commission on AIDS. *The Challenge of HIV/AIDS in Communities of Color* (1992); U.S. National Commission on AIDS. *Failure of the U.S. Health Care System to Deal with HIV Epidemic* (1989); U.S. National Commission on AIDS. *Report of the Working Group on Social/Human Issues* (1990); World Health Organisation. *Global AIDS News*, no.1 (1993).

23 THE COSTS OF CARE

It is a well known fact that the U.S. health care system is the most expensive in the world, but the benefits to Americans are not all that clear. In 1992, over 37 million people, or 15 percent of the population, were without health insurance for the entire year; at any given moment, however, the total is much higher. Though the uninsured come in all colors and demographic groups, they are most likely to be adults between 18 and 34, black or Hispanic, and poor – but working. The nonworking poor are frequently covered by Medicaid. One of the cruelties of the American job-based system of health coverage is that people often lose their insurance when they go off welfare to take a low-paying job. Even year-round, full-time work is no guarantee of coverage; 12% of such fully employed workers were uninsured for all of 1992. Men are less likely to be covered than women (13% vs. 16%). The only group shielded from the risk of uninsurance is the elderly: more than 98% of those over age 65 are covered, mainly by Medicare. Every other country in the rich world covers virtually all its citizens – and devotes a smaller share of national income to health.

The lack of value-for-money in U.S. health spending can also be measured in poor outcomes, like shorter life expectancies and higher infant mortality rates than the rest of the rich world. These are, however, probably more a function of poverty than medical care in the narrow sense. Evidence for that can be found in the fact that death rates decline with rising income. However income alone cannot explain everything. As the graphic shows, death rates for blacks are higher than those for whites even in the same income class; the heritage of racism has to be contributing to this disparity.

Why is the U.S. system so costly? It is hard to point to a single factor. Though medical specialization and high-tech interventions are emphasized rather than primary health care, the mix of clinical expenditures – the share going to providers' salaries, drugs, equipment, and so on – is similar to that in other industrial countries. But each element, it seems, is more expensive in the U.S. Administrative overhead is far higher as well; over a thousand insurance companies provide health coverage, each with different forms and procedures, requiring doctors and hospitals to maintain huge billing staffs. Though Americans are accustomed to associating bureaucratic inefficiencies with government, this administrative maze is largely private. Overhead accounts for 12% of private insurers' costs, compared with 3% for Medicare and Medicaid – and the public sector's costs are inflated by processing contracts with private firms who charge the U.S.

government nearly seven times what it costs the Canadian government to process a claim. Likely health reforms will probably retain a large role for private insurance companies, possibly even grafting new supervisory layers on them, which may do little to reduce administrative costs. But high administrative costs do not tell the whole story. According to the O.E.C.D., U.S. doctors' salaries are 5.5 times average earnings, compared with 4 times in Germany, 3.5 in Canada, and 2.5 in Japan.

Sources to the map:
Eisenberg, David M., Ronald C. Kessler, Cindy Foster, Frances E. Norlock, David R. Calkins, and Thomas L. Delbanco. "Unconventional Medicine in the United States: Prevalence, Costs, and Patterns of Use." *New England Journal of Medicine*, no. 328 (28 January 1993): 246–252; Organisation for Economic Cooperation and Development. *OECD in Figures: Statistics on the Member Countries, 1993* (supplement to the *OECD Observer*, June–July 1993); Organisation for Economic Cooperation and Development. *U.S. Health Care at the Cross-Roads*. Paris: OECD, 1992; Pappas, Gregory. Prevention magazine. *The Prevention Index: Summary Report, 1993*. Emmaus, PA: Rodale Press, 1993; U.S. Bureau of the Census. Cendata computer database, through Compuserve Information Service, Columbus, Ohio; U.S. Bureau of the Census. "Poverty in the United States, 1992." *Current Population Reports*, Series P60-185 (September 1993) Washington, D.C., 1993; U.S. Bureau of the Census. *Statistical Abstract of the United States: 1993*. Washington, D.C.; U.S. National Center for Health Statistics. *Health United States 1992* (August 1993); Woolhandler, Steffie and David U. Himmelstein. "The Deteriorating Administrative Efficiency of the U.S. Health Care System." *New England Journal of Medicine*, no. 324 (2 May 1991): 1253–1258.

24 ABORTION

Obstacles to abortion, in the U.S. and elsewhere in the world, are surprisingly recent. Although abortion has not always been seen as unambiguously acceptable, the view of abortion as murder was virtually unknown until the late 19th century. But, as Kristin Luker says in her strikingly dispassionate study of the subject, "throughout most of the history of Western Christianity, abortion early in pregnancy, though verbally chastized [sic], was often legally ignored." Early American law continued this tradition of looking the other way. Various contemporary studies estimated that one-quarter to one-third of all 19th-century pregnancies ended in abortion. The figure for 1988 was 25.1 percent.

The American right-to-life movement, Luker shows, was founded by physicians who wanted to shut down nonmedical abortionists. (The early motivation of today's prochoice movement was ironically the same.) In 1859, the 12-year-old American Medical Association, passed a resolution condemning abortion. The campaign was central to their efforts to improve the status and power of the medical profession. The goal was to shift its control to MDs, by convincing a skeptical public that abortion, as well as being morally wrong, was dangerous at the hand of nonprofessionals.

By 1900, most states had shifted the decision-making power to doctors; abortion would be illegal in all cases except when necessary to save the life of the mother, and physicians would be the sole judges of such "therapeutic necessity." Of course, many women obtained illegal abortions, often at appalling risk. But it was not until the feminist and sexual revolutions of the 1960s that the legal status of abortion came under challenge. Those challenges culminated in the U.S. Supreme Court's 1973 decision Roe v. Wade , which prohibited states from outlawing abortions during the first six months. Ironically, despite the impression in anti-abortion circles, that this was a radical decision, it merely restored the standards prevailing in the 19th century. And with abortion now legal, the abortion rate – one pregnancy in four ending in induced abortion – has returned to 19th-century levels. But, in another irony, pro-choice advocates now defend physician abortionists, and dread the return of the non-credentialled kind, should Roe v. Wade ever be overturned.

For the moment Roe v. Wade seems legally secure, with a pro-choice President who is not likely to appoint a Supreme Court Justice who would vote to overturn the decision. For many women abortion may be legal, but obtaining one may be near impossible financially or geographically. Only a dozen states permit Medicaid funding for abortions for the indigent. About 80 percent of U.S. counties and almost a quarter of all metropolitan areas have no provider. Vilification and violence against doctors and clinics means that some doctors are refusing to offer the procedure. In 1993, one doctor was murdered for performing abortions, and a quarter of all clinics suffered some form of violence in the first seven months of the year.

Consequently, many women have to travel to get abortions, because they are unavailable closer to home. In 1985, over a quarter of the women seeking abortions in Arkansas, Indiana, Kentucky, Maryland, Mississippi, West Virginia, and Wyoming traveled out of state for them. While the "pro-life" movement has apparently lost the legal battle, they have succeeded in rendering the legal status of abortion moot across much of the U.S.

Sources to the map:
Alan Guttmacher Institute. "70 U.S. Metropolitan Areas Have No Abortion Provider." press release (21 May 1992) New York City, 1992; Feminist Majority Foundation. *1993 Clinic Violence Survey Report.* Arlington, VA, 1993; Henshaw, Stanley K. and Jennifer Van Vort. "Abortion Services in the United States, 1987 and 1988." *Family Planning Perspectives,* no. 22 (May/June 1990):102-108, 142; Luker, Kristen. *Abortion and the Politics of Motherhood.* Berkeley and Los Angeles: University of California Press, 1984; National Abortion Rights Action League. *Who Decides: A State-by-State Review of Abortion Rights.* Washington, D.C.: NARAL, 1993.

25 GAYS AND THE LAW

Public attitudes towards gay men and lesbians are deeply contradictory. Polls have repeatedly shown that over four-fifths of the American public thinks sexual relations between members of the same sex is morally wrong. And the feelings thermometer shows that homosexuals are not regarded warmly. This disapproval takes legal form in anti-sodomy laws, which, though rarely enforced, are nonetheless a visible measure of public hostility.

On the other hand, opinion polls also show a surprisingly large majority of Americans opposed to discrimination on the basis of sexual preference. A considerable number of states, counties, and cities have enacted laws granting some degree of protection to lesbians and gay men – protections ranging from narrowly drawn statutes covering public employees to broadly drawn ones granting a full array of civil rights protections covering employment, housing, credit, and public accommodation. Numerous jurisdictions and private employers are also beginning to grant health and other benefits to the partners of their gay and lesbian employees. This contradiction reaches its strangest point in Minnesota, which has both an anti-sodomy law and a state civil rights law protecting homosexuals.

The maps make clear the geographical pattern of (in)tolerance. The South and Mountain states are not friendly environments for people who love members of their own sex. The friendliest jurisdictions are in California, the Northeast, and the upper Midwest. Big cities, university towns, and high-tech enclaves are the friendliest localities.

A backlash is developing against legal protections. The religious right has been succeeding in its campaign against homosexuals by getting measures through that would prevent localities from passing civil rights laws placed on state ballots. This happened in Colorado in 1992. The right's rhetorical strategy has been to argue that gays and lesbians are seeking "special privileges," not guarantees of non-discrimination, and this appeal has won some converts. Whatever the results in the short term, the battle is likely to continue in the courts and in referenda for years to come.

Sources to the map:
American National Election Study. University of Michigan: Ann Arbor, MI, 1992; National Gay and Lesbian Task Force. Washington, D.C.; Sherrill, Kenneth. "Half Empty: Gay Power and Gay Powerlessness in American Politics." Paper presented at the Annual Meeting of the American Political Science Association, Washington, D.C., August 1991.

Acknowledgments
Mark Hertzog of the University of Virginia, Ken Sherrill and L.D. Stratton of Bradley University for their friendly assistance, and to the Queer Resources Directory, a computer database, for simplifying my research.

26 THE FAT OF THE LAND

American eating habits have become world-famous, from the Golden Arches to various postmodern nutritional obsessions. The U.S. has turned dieting and calorie counting into major industries – and exported them worldwide. But the latest evidence on eating habits, while apparently conflicting, shows that indulgence, never fully out of style, may be regaining the upper hand.

One of the more striking changes of the last 20 years is the sharp decline in beef consumption, and a compensatory rise in fish and poultry eating. Consumption of fresh vegetables and fruit is also up about as much as red meat-eating is down. Clearly this has something to do with the long-term decline in dietary cholesterol, which makes for healthier circulatory systems.

But the news on other dietary habits is quite mixed. Health authorities advise that no more than 30 percent of daily calorie intake should come from fats, preferably less. Substantial progress has been made along those lines. The fat share of dietary calories fell from 42% in the 1960s, to 36% in 1978, to 34% in 1990. But unfortunately, this decline has resulted not only from a fall in the numerator (fats) but also an increase in the denominator (total calories). So while people are eating less fat, they are then eating more calories, and getting notably fatter.

Most alarming for future health is the fact that young adults are leading the way to greater corpulence. Between 1985–86 and 1992–93, the average weight for people aged 25–30 rose from 161 pounds to 171. One can speculate on the reasons why, but it is striking that men get fatter as income rises, while women tend to become slimmer. Men and women, blacks and whites, all got heavier – though blood cholesterol levels declined. Researchers speculate that people are exercising less and substituting carbohydrates for fats – potato chips, pretzels, and cheese worms no doubt prominent among them.

According to trend maven Faith Popcorn, proprietor of the New York-based market research firm BrainReserve, these trends are likely to continue through the decade. As of late 1993, only a third of Americans got "strenuous" exercise, down four points from 1991. Between the late 1980s and the early 1990s, pork consumption rose, and fat and cholesterol avoidance fell. McDonald's is planning to roll out a Mega Mac, a half-pound gutbuster that is the opposite of the 1980s innovation, the low-fat McLean pattie. Popcorn calls this the "pleasure revenge."

Indulgence can be bad news for the environment as well. According to the Columbia Basin Institute, frozen french fries have ravaged the Pacific Northwest, where 80 percent of the American supply is produced, most of it destined for fast food palaces. Producers discard about half the potato to assure uniform shapes. That waste, plus the tankloads of chemicals used on the crop, have so polluted the area that direct application of local water can burn the plants, and a third of residential wells violate federal standards. And despite promises of high-wage work, the industry has created a rural underclass of badly paid and irregularly employed migrant workers, mainly Hispanics. All this has been done with decades of heavy federal, state, and local subsidies. The plants are reportedly so foul that journalists are not allowed to visit them.

Sources to the map:
Associated Press. "Weight of Average Young U.S. Adult Rose 10 Pounds in Seven-Year Period." *Wall Street Journal* (18 March 1994): B7A; Bean, William and David Runsten.*Value Added and Subtracted: The Processed Potato Industry in the Mid-Columbia Basin*. Portland, OR: Columbia Basin Institute, 1994; Brody, Jane E. "Americans Reducing Fat in Diet." *New York Times* (8 March 1994): C6; Popcorn, Faith. Unpublished data. New York: BrainReserve; Snack Food Association. *Consumer Snacking Behavior Report*. Alexandria, VA, 1992; Snack Food Association. *State of the Industry Report*. Alexandria, VA, 1993; U.S. Centers for Disease Control. *Morbidity and Mortality Weekly Report*, no.43 (25 February 1994):7; U.S. National Center for Health Statistics. *Health Promotion and Disease Prevention: United States, 1990* (April 1993).

27 CRIME

No other rich industrial country – and, though the social statistics of the poor world may be less than reliable, probably no other country at all – has a crime rate as high as the USA's, and no other country jails so many of its citizens. But one reason the jail population is increasing so rapidly is that the public is convinced that criminality is soaring. This is not so.

Take, for example, murder, which is not only the gravest of crimes, but the one for which the best statistics are available. Compared with other serious crimes, like rape and robbery, the police have a pretty good idea of the number of people who meet a violent end. And although the murder rate has doubled since the early 1960s – from 5 per 100,000 to 9–10 today – most of that doubling happened during the 1960s and early 1970s. Since then, the murder rate has stayed relatively steady. This is 9–10 per 100,000 too high, but it is not the rising trend so often cited.

The numbers for other crimes are far spongier. Beyond the problem of inconsistent reporting of crimes to the police, there is also the problem of inconsistent reporting by the police – specifically, not all departments fill out the forms filed with the FBI with equal competence or care. That makes comparison of crime rates across time or jurisdictions very difficult.

The statistics on the map are police statistics, since for state crime rates there are no other figures available. A better source for national statistics – as it would be for state statistics, were they available, would have been the National Crime Victimization Survey (NCVS), a poll that the Justice Department has been conducting since 1973. The NCVS asks people if they have been victims of a crime during the survey period, and if so, what kind. Since the survey's methodology has been consistent throughout its history, it is a more reliable guide to trends. And it also asks questions about race, place of residence, and income, thereby giving a good picture of the demographics of crime.

According to the NCVS, the violent crime rate has been virtually flat for the last 20 years, and nonviolent household offenses like break-ins have declined. During the same period, the incarceration rate has more than tripled. Roughly one in 30 adults is victimized by a violent crime (rape, robbery, and assault) every year. Again, this is one in 30 too high, but the trend is flat. The risk of victimization itself must be put in perspective: someone is half again as likely to be injured at work than to be the victim of a violent crime; twice as likely to be hurt in a car crash as injured by a criminal; and four times as likely to die in an auto wreck as at the hand of a murderer.

As with health, wealth, and wisdom, the averages in the U.S. conceal an inequitable distribution of victims. NCVS figures show that the poor and the nonwhite are far more likely to be targets of a violent crime than the affluent and white. Blacks are roughly four times as likely to be murder victims as whites – meaning that while the white murder rate is roughly on a par with that of France (yet three times that of Japan), the black murder rate is like nothing else seen in the northern hemisphere, and probably the southern as well. For crimes against property, the risks are roughly equal – a curious egalitarianism, considering that the poor and nonwhite have, on average, a lot less to steal.

Why is the U.S. so violent? An alleged epidemic of bastardy is an explanation favored by maiNstream analysts and politicians, but international comparisons do not bear this out (**20 Families**). Twice as many Swedish births occur without the blessings of the state as American, but Sweden is one of the most peaceful countries on earth. Canada's "illegitimacy" rate is about the same as the U.S.'s, but their crime rate is a fraction of the American crime rate. Better explanations would include poverty, social decay, and an inherited culture of violence.

Sources to the map:
U.S. Bureau of Justice Statistics. *Sourcebook of Criminal Justice Statistics: 1992.* Washington, D.C., 1992; The Sentencing Project. *Young Black Men and the Criminal Justice System.* Washington, D.C., 1990.

Acknowledgment
Thanks to Tony Pate, research director of the Police Foundation, Washington, D.C., for his long, thoughtful memo clarifying the differences among the crime statistics.

28 SANCTIONED KILLING

In executing people for ordinary crimes – offenses other than treason during wartime – the U.S. keeps some unexpected company. No countries in Western Europe and only a handful in Latin America still use the death penalty. The only other First World country that takes the lives of criminals is Japan. This is done secretly, often on only several hours notice to the prisoner.

All methods of execution have their horrors. The executed always lose sphincter control and executioners now use diapers and plugs. Contrary to popular assumption, hanging does not bring instant death; the hanged gasp and writhe as their neck is crushed. Electrocution, once offered as an improvement on hanging, cooks the prisoner; the eyes pop out of their sockets, and the skin sometimes bursts into flame. The gas chamber was introduced as a humane improvement on electrocution but its victims experience seizures and are thought to feel pain like that of an intense heart attack. Lethal injection, the latest "improvement", is not without its horrors. Since it is hard to find doctors who will administer the fatal jab, it is left to technicians, often poorly trained, who can poke about for up to an hour in search of a suitable vein. For those executed, even the most painless finale comes after an average of seven years has been spent on death row. Since capital punishment was resumed in the U.S. in 1977 only one woman has been executed; death row is 98.8 percent male.

As Thomas Paine once asked "Why is it that scarcely any are executed but the poor?" For crimes no more horrid than those of more affluent thugs who escape with mere jailtime, prisoners sentenced to die are usually too poor to afford decent counsel and expert witnesses. Race matters too. Though the evidence is not conclusive, blacks seem more likely to draw a death sentence than whites. Nevertheless it has been proven that killers of whites are far more likely to draw a death sentence than killers of blacks.

While the number of murders has not quite doubled in the last 25 years, the death row population has grown by over 400 percent. At the present rate of nearly 40 executions a year, it would take over 70 years to eliminate everyone on death row – and 10 or 20 years just to execute the annual new arrivals. Just under four percent of the prisoners who have received death sentences since 1977 have been executed. A third have their sentences lifted, but the remaining population continues to grow. Either the death penalty must be lifted or the pace of execution must increase exponentially – and the Supreme Court has been doing its bit to speed the pace by "deregulating" the death penalty, making it ever-harder to lodge an appeal. As it is, the U.S. is creating a strange underworld of people condemned to die who merely languish indefinitely.

There is no credible evidence that capital punishment deters crime. The U.S. has by far the highest murder rate of the rich world. States with capital punishment do not enjoy lower murder rates than those without it, according to the American Civil Liberties Union, and states that have introduced or renounced the death penalty show no change in their crime rate. But the death penalty remains popular. New states are joining the execution roster all the time, and over 500 prisoners await death in states that have conducted no executions in 25 years.

Sources to the map:
American Civil Liberties Union. "The Death Penalty." ACLU Briefing Paper, no.8 (no date) New York; Amnesty International. "United States of America: Death Penalty Developments in 1992." AMR 51/25/93 (April 1993); Amnesty International. "The Death Penalty: List of Abolitionist and Retentionist Countries." ACT 500/04/93 (June 1993); Amnesty International. "USA: More Juvenile Offenders Face Execution Following Supreme Court Ruling." AMR 51/WU 07/93 (6 July 1993); Death Penalty Information Center. "Facts About the Death Penalty." (11 August) Washington, D.C., 1993; Kaminer, Wendy. "Radelet, Bedau, and Putnam's *In Spite of Innocence: Erroneous Convictions in Capital Cases.*" *Atlantic Monthly* (December 1992); Merrill, Michael. "Peter Linebaugh's *The London Hanged: Crime and Civil Society in the Eighteenth Century.*" *Nation* (22 June 1992); National Coalition to Abolish the Death Penalty. *Methods of Execution.* Washington, D.C., 1993; U.S. Bureau of Justice Statistics. *Capital Punishment 1991.* Washington, D.C., 1991; U.S. Bureau of Justice Statistics. *Sourcebook 1991.* Washington, D.C., 1991; U.S. General Accounting Office. *Death Penalty Sentencing: Research Indicates Pattern of Racial Disparities* GAO/GGD-90-57 (February 1990) Washington, D.C., 1990; Weisberg, Jacob. "This Is Your Death: Capital Punishment – What Really Happens." *New Republic* (1 July 1991).

29 IN GOD WE TRUST

Has there ever been a country, formal theocracies excepted, where religion played a larger role in public and private life than the U.S.A.? In 1991, nearly 9 in 10 Americans (89%) told Times Mirror pollsters that they never doubted the existence of God; only Poles (87%) and Italians (80%) came close to this figure. Only 59% of Germans reported such unwavering faith, 58% of the British, 47% of the French, and 46% of Russians. When it comes to the hereafter, the contrasts are sharper; 71% of Americans told

Gallup pollsters in 1979 they believed in an afterlife; just under half of the Italians, Dutch, Australians, and British agreed, and only 39% of West Germans. And those Americans who believe that death is only a transition, not an end, show a great deal of confidence that they will prosper in the afterworld, a confidence that our Puritan forbears might find unseemly. Curiously, more Americans believe in heaven than hell, and have done so throughout 40 years of polling; heaven is a better proposition.

In spite of this deep attachment to religion, few hard figures on denominational affiliation were available until two researchers at the City University of New York, Barry Kosmin and Seymour Lachman, conducted a National Survey of Religious Identification (NSRI) in 1990. The Census Bureau flirted with a religious survey in 1957, but opposition from Jews, Christian Scientists, and civil liberties groups forced them to drop the plan, never to revive it. Churches do issue estimates of their adherents, but coverage is spotty and the numbers are unreliable.

Scrutiny of the NSRI data, presented in Kosmin and Lachman's *One Nation Under God*, reveals that while there is an amazing diversity of religious identification among Americans, almost all that diversity is Christian. Over 86% of adults called themselves Christians, though over 40 denominations showed up on the survey. Jews accounted for just under 2%, and those calling themselves agnostics or nonreligious, for 8%. Leaving aside the 2.3% who refused to answer, that left only 1.5% who belonged to all other religions – Muslim, Buddhist, Unitarian, Scientologist, New Age, Wiccan, and the rest. (While 10–20% of the public expresses some interest in "New Age" beliefs, many adapt them to their mainstream religion – and many more are hostile to the movement.) Given the great ethnic diversity of the country, the rarity of non-Judeo-Christian religions is surprising.

While it is sometimes thought that religion is on the wane, this is not borne out by the polls. For example, the share of the population reporting that they believe in heaven and hell is higher in the 1990s than it was in the 1950s or early 1960s. Also, an average of 31 Gallup polls taken between 1986 and 1993 shows a steady rise in the percentage share of the population calling themselves born-again or evangelical Christians, from the low-30s in 1986 to the mid-40s in 1993. Nor, as the graphic shows clearly, does religious broadcasting show any signs of dying out. As it says on the currency, In God We Trust.

Sources to the map:
Gallup Poll data, through the Roper Center's Public Opinion On-Line (POLL) computer database; Kosmin, Barry A. and Seymour P. Lachman. *One Nation Under God: Religion in Contemporary American Society*. New York: Harmony Books, 1993; National Religious Broadcasters. *Directory of Religious Broadcasting 1992–1993*. Manassas, VA: NRB, 1993; "Times Mirror Center for People and the Press." Data reported in *Los Angeles Times* (17 September 1991).

30 THE CONSCIOUSNESS INDUSTRY

One thing is for certain – like most other business sectors, the media business is getting more concentrated. Over the last several years, vast mergers, notably Time with Warner and Paramount (parent of Simon & Schuster) with Viacom (parent of MTV), have created multimedia conglomerates with a global reach. The business rationale for these combinations, outside of the normal lust for bigness, is that the new firms will be able to offer great synergies: a novel published by one branch of MegaMedia could be excerpted in a magazine published by another, made into a movie by yet another, with the movie then shown on the firm's cable TV division.

Critics of this concentration view the trend with alarm, but size alone bears no determinate relation with quality. For example, only a handful of American cities now have more than one newspaper, but the resident of New York, one of the exceptions, must wonder about the value of competition in journalism. Compared to Britain, whose newspaper market is dominated by fewer than a dozen national titles, the U.S. market is a font of diversity – but in many ways the "quality" British papers are far better than the American ones. What may be the best American newspaper, the *Wall Street Journal*, is national in scope but it has little serious competition. Quality might be better served by a few national papers rather than a thousand local monopolies. Sentiment over individual ownership does not bear too much examination. The *Los Angeles Times* – a newspaper that was once little more than a cheerleading sheet for the Chandler family's real estate interests – did not become a serious enterprise until it was put under professional management and began to turn itself into a conglomerate.

U.S. media penetration abroad is, admittedly, powerful; Hollywood movies draw more Europeans than do locally produced films, and Michael Jackson T-shirts can be spotted around the world. But after decades of such one-way traffic, the flow is now reversing somewhat: Japan's Sony owns CBS Records and Columbia Pictures; Matsushita (also of Japan) owns MCA; Germany's Bertelsman owns Bantam Doubleday Dell and RCA Records; and Britain's Pearson owns Viking–Penguin. The culture industry is being increasingly conglomeratized, but it is becoming multinational as well.

Sources to the map:
Broadcasting & Cable Yearbook 1993. New York: Broadcasting & Cable Inc., 1993; Cable News Network press office citing Nielsen research for the U.S. and AGB Media Metered Viewing Data – The Netherlands for international figures. Conversation with the author (January 1994); *Editor & Publisher 1993 Yearbook.* New York: Editor & Publisher Inc., 1993; Gale Research. *Gale Directory of Publications and Broadcast Media.* Detroit, MI: Gale Research, Inc., 1993; MTV. "MTV Worldwide Reach Estimates." (December 1993); Standard & Poors. Corporate reports, through Compustat and S & P Online computer databases.

Acknowledgment:
Phil Mattera of the National Writers Union who provided a list of the Newhouse holdings. Newhouse is a privately owned corporation that refused to provide any information about its empire.

Part Four
GOVERNMENT

These nine groupings of the American polity come from the Times Mirror Center for The People & The Press, a Washington-based public opinion research group owned by the Los Angeles-based media conglomerate (see **30 The Consciousness Industry**.) They are based on answers to poll questions designed to reveal "nine basic values and orientations," party affiliation, and the degree of political involvement. The exercise was first performed in 1990, and the number of groupings was initially 11; these were reduced to nine in 1992.

The classifications are a little facile, as any attempt to capture a person's political philosophy in a single word must be, or any attempt to fit 186 million adults into nine categories. For example, the typology makes no room for radicals of the right or left. And the system is now showing signs of age now that the Cold War is over. All reservations aside, the classifications are still enlightening.

One use of the typology is to clarify what happened in the 1992 election. Upbeats, who loved Ronald Reagan, were much less enthusiastic about George Bush. Disaffecteds, whom Bush carried in 1988, shifted over to Bill Clinton in 1992; and Ross Perot raided the Enterprisers, a formerly solid GOP constituency. At the same time, Clinton held on to core Democratic groups, and even scooped up the Bystanders.

Source:
Times Mirror Center for The People & The Press, Washington, D.C.: *The People, The Press & Politics 1990: A Times Mirror Political Typology* (October 11, 1990), and *The People, The Press and Politics: Campaign '92: Voters Say "Thumbs Up!" To Campaign, Process & Coverage* (November 15, 1992).

31 ALL POLITICS IS LOCAL

There is one government in the U.S. for every 3,000 people – quite a lot for a country that is less than keen on government. State and local governments account for a larger share of total public spending than any Group of Seven country save Canada, but most of Canada's sub-federal spending is done by provinces, not localities; in the U.S., spending by state and local governments is roughly equal. Does this result in an inefficient duplication of efforts? Or does it assure that the governors will stay close to the governed, and that a healthy competition will prevail among jurisdictions to assure the best services will be delivered at the lowest possible cost?

In general, the more governments a state has, the more government workers it has (relative to its population). This makes intuitive sense. A police department or planning board would not have to double in size if the population in its charge doubled; there are certain economies of scale in any enterprise, even government. But the relation is far from iron-clad, since the number of government employees depends not only on the number of governments, but on what services those governments offer their citizens as well.

The struggle over the form of local government goes back over a century. Many cities annexed their suburbs in the late 19th century in the interests of efficiency. But targeted localities increasingly resisted absorption, leading reformers to invent the "special district" to handle water supply, transportation, land use planning, and other important activities. The politics of these conflicts are complex and undemocratic – on both sides. Consolidators were often anti-democratic technocrats, who wanted to weaken the power of urban ethnic and working class populations, and home-rule anticonsolidators were often trying to wall themselves off from the same teeming hordes. Special districts could finesse some of these problems, but they could easily be dominated by various special interests more interested in promoting profitable real estate development than the public interest. Where the water or sewer or train lines went could determine which tracts of land were to flourish, and which not.

Remarkably little has changed in this dynamic in 70 years – technocrats would love to see more regional approaches to planning, but suburban residents want to protect their fiefdoms. Sprawling areas like New Jersey, Long Island, and Greater Los Angeles face profound regional social and ecological problems, but every town wants to preserve its sovereignty while evading any fiscal responsibility for the region's poor. Suburbanites, who have enjoyed decades of subsidies, from highway building to a home mortgage interest which is tax deductible, balk at the idea of sharing their wealth or their schools with impoverished urbanites. The defense of "home rule" in the 1990s still means, as it did in the 1920s, separating "us" and "them."

Ironically, many special districts have been quite successful at their specified tasks, like running a highway or a water district, thereby reducing pressures for broader political integration and more comprehensive planning. And these narrow successes can also bring about broader failures – a successful highway, like the New Jersey Turnpike, also stimulates sprawl and smog; a successful water district, like that in Los Angeles, can bring overdevelopment. On the other hand, the panoply of state and local governments stimulates bidding wars to see which jurisdiction can offer the lowest taxes and loosest regulations in order to attract businesses – a war of each against all that does little to stimulate real economic development, but does put footloose managers in a mighty bargaining position.

Finally, is localism efficient? Here is a provocative measure offered in lieu of an answer: the U.S. has about the same share of its workforce employed in the public sector (14.4%) as Germany (14.8%) and Italy (15.5%) – countries that most Americans probably regard as choking on government.

Sources to the map:
International Monetary Fund. *Government Finance Statistics Yearbook 1992*. Washington, D.C.: IMF, 1992; Organisation for Economic Cooperation and Development. *OECD in Figures 1993* (supplement to the *OECD Observer*, June–July 1993). U.S. Bureau of the Census. Cendata computer database, through Compuserve Information Service, Columbus, Ohio; U.S. Bureau of the Census. *Government Finances 1989–90*, Series GF/90-5 (December 1991) Washington, D.C., 1991; U.S. Bureau of the Census. *Statistical Abstract of the United States: 1993*. Washington, D.C., 1993.

Acknowledgment:
Sarah Elkind of the University of Michigan for an excellent overview of the regionalization struggle, past and present.

32 THE PERMANENT GOVERNMENT

Years ago, only radicals made the argument that elected officials were subordinate to a permanent government of lawyers, corporate lobbyists, and rich campaign contributors.

In recent years, though, this has become a pretty mainstream idea. And no wonder – their influence grows and grows.

Congress, as well as most local legislatures, is dominated by lawyers, who write laws that can only be decoded and applied by other lawyers. Virtually every aspect of American life, from birth to marriage to death, is charmed by their touch. Fees paid to lawyers and their employees swelled from 0.2% of gross domestic product (GDP) in 1962 – the same as 1952 and 1929 – to 0.9% in 1992, and 1.4% in 1992, a sevenfold increase.

There is no greater concentration of lawyers anywhere in the U.S., and probably on earth, than Washington, D.C. There, they interpret, litigate, and plead on behalf of their clients, typically corporations and other interest groups eager to bend federal power towards their own enrichment. Many of the District's 32,000 lawyers have nothing to do with Perry Masonish pursuits; their real task is persuading Congress and regulators to pass new laws to promote their interests or to stop proposed laws that threaten them. The relationship can get quite intimate. For decades, to take an important example, legislation affecting savings & loans was essentially written by industry lawyer-lobbyists. The resulting indulgence of the laws contributed greatly to the industry's eventual crisis and subsequent federal bailout which will end up costing U.S. taxpayers $250 billion. They earned this law-writing privilege by contributing generously to the political campaigns of key Congress people.

This introduces the other focus of these pages, the campaign funders. Shown are two of the crucial sources of political dollars – "soft money," which are lightly regulated contributions by corporations, rich individuals, and other monied interests to the national party headquarters, and political action committee (PAC) contributions, given mainly to Congressional candidates. Note that the overwhelming source of such funds are business interests; labor unions, often depicted as thuggish influence peddlers, look like pikers next to employers. Note too that the Democrats, supposedly the party of the little guy, have no problem raising funds from the big guys. In fact, about the only difference between the parties revealed by the bar charts is that the Democrats get more from labor, Hollywood, and pro-Israel groups than the Republicans – mere pocket change by Washington standards.

Sources to the map:
Center for Public Integrity. Washington, D.C.; Curran, Barbara and Clara N. Carson, eds. *The U.S. Legal Profession in 1988.* Chicago: American Bar Foundation, 1988; Goldstein, Josh. *Soft Money, Real Dollars: Soft Money in the 1992 Elections.* Center for Responsive Politics, Washington, D.C., 1993; Makinson, Larry. *The Price of Admission: Campaign Spending in the 1992 Elections.* Center for Responsive Politics, Washington, D.C., 1993; U.S. Bureau of the Census. *Statistical Abstract of the United States: 1993.* Washington, D.C., 1993.

Acknowledgment:
Center for Responsive Politics for transforming Federal Election Commission records into accessible form, and for their generosity and courtesy.

33 THE ELECTED GOVERNMENT

While the presidential election of 1992 represented a departure from the previous three elections, it hardly qualified as a landslide, or even a realignment of political loyalties of lasting significance. The Republicans share of the vote fell by 13 percentage points between 1980 and 1992, but the Democrats gained only 2 points from that shift, with the balance going to independent candidates, mainly Ross Perot. Despite running a Southern and relatively conservative candidate, the Democrats lost ground in the south, and made significant gains mainly in the West. Democratic leaders who hoped the renunciation of the party's liberal heritage would gain votes in these conservative areas have yet to prove their case.

President Clinton was elected with the support of 24% of the voting age population, not just the lowest share of any winning candidate since 1960, as shown in our graphic, but lower than any share since Calvin Coolidge picked up 24% in 1924. But even elections now remembered as landslides did not produce overwhelming numbers. Lyndon

B. Johnson won in 1964 with just 38%, slightly more than Franklin Roosevelt's 35% in 1936. Reagan's victories of 1980 and 1984, both repeatedly called landslides by many analysts, were accomplished with 27% and 31% respectively. The major reason for these unimpressive numbers is low voter turnout (**34 Democracy in America**); how much does getting 60% of the vote really mean if 40% of the potential electorate stays home?

The stranglehold that white men have had on Congress is loosening somewhat. The 103rd Congress, elected in 1992, is the most diverse ever. Even so, the makeup of the national legislature, especially the Senate, is a long way from reflecting the demographics of the national population. But how can a body that is 45% attorneys reflect a national population?

Sources to the map:
Amer, Mildred L. *Membership of the 103d Congress: A Profile.* Washington, D.C.: Library of Congress, 1993; U.S. Bureau of the Census. *Statistical Abstract of the United States:1993.* Washington, D.C., 1993; U.S. Bureau of the Census. *Historical Statistics of the United States, Colonial Times to 1970.* Washington, D.C., 1976.

34 DEMOCRACY IN AMERICA

If participation in elections – registration and voting – is an important measure of democracy, then democracy in America is none too healthy. It was considered a cause for celebration that 55 percent of the voting age population turned out to vote in November 1992, the best performance in 20 years. But as the flags graphic shows, even this swell in participation leaves the U.S. near the bottom of international rankings.

Why is American turnout so low? An answer popular among political conservatives is that the population is basically pleased with things as they are, and sees no great reason to vote. But the opposite may hold more truth – that there is nothing to vote for.

The demographic picture of (non) voting does not support the mass happiness argument. The likelihood of voting rises with income, meaning that the electorate is disproportionally rich and white, the very people most likely to be pleased with the status quo. About 26% of adults have incomes over $35,000; 34% have incomes under $20,000. But their shares of the electorate are almost precisely reversed: 32% for adults with incomes over $35,000, and 26% for those with incomes under $20,000.

This profile of the voting and abstaining populations is highly imperfect. While very good estimates of the voting age population and the number of votes cast are available, discovering who votes and who does not can only be done by surveys of the sort conducted by the Census Bureau. It is well known that people tend to tell pollsters what they want to hear; since it is considered embarrassing not to vote, more people tell Census surveyors that they did vote than actually did. So, an actual turnout of 55% in the 1992 election became a 62% turnout in the Census' voting report. Even more confusing, the Census Bureau figures that the poorer people are, the more they are likely to report having voted when they did not. So the actual electorate is probably even more skewed than the figures reported here.

Total voting age population figures, including both citizens and noncitizens, have been used in the maps and graphics. The Census Bureau, with good reason, does not have much confidence in the accuracy of figures for non-citizens. And noncitizens, who cannot vote, still pay taxes, and obey the laws. This partly explains the extraordinarily low turnouts for Hispanics and Asians/Pacific Islanders. If numbers for citizens alone were used (however spongy), the percentages voting would be as follows: 67% of whites; 57% of blacks; 50% of Asian/Pacific Islanders; 47% of Hispanics.

Since noncitizens have lower incomes on average, using only citizens would make the turnout by income chart look less lopsided. But it seems important that a large portion of the U.S. population – 7 percent of all adults – consists of noncitizens who are excluded from political life.

Sources to the map:
Gans, Curtis. Committee for the Study of the American Electorate, Washington, D.C.; Jennings, Jerry T. "Voting and Registration in the Election of November 1992." *Current Population Reports*, P20-466 (April 1993) Washington, D.C.: U.S. Bureau of the Census, 1993; U.S. Bureau of the Census. Cendata computer database, through Compuserve Information Service, Columbus, Ohio; U.S. Bureau of the Census. *Statistical Abstract of the United States: 1993*. Washington, D.C., 1993.

35 THE PENTAGON

The U.S. is now the world's only remaining superpower, responsible for about half the world's military spending. Yet before the U.S.S.R., its undeclared enemy and the opposing superpower, dissolved, the U.S. share of world military spending was only 29 percent.

The U.S. retains a global network of bases and fleets, the likes of which the world never saw before the Cold War. But despite an apparent increase in responsibility, the superpower is pulling back. Bases are being closed, not only in Europe, where the threat of a Soviet invasion is no longer pressing, but in the U.S. as well. While the Pentagon budget remains more or less steady in dollar terms, it is steadily shrinking as a share of gross domestic product (GDP), and will soon claim the smallest share of the economy since before World War II. These cutbacks have brought hardship to the regions and occupations that once thrived on the permanent war economy.

Ironically, those regions include some of the most conservative – which usually translates into anti-government – parts of the country. Southern California, the spiritual home of the anti-tax rebellions of the 1970s, would not exist in its present form without decades of military contracts. So too with whole industries, like computers and micro-electronics, centers of self-reliant libertarian ideology and myths of the heroic entrepreneur. In all but name, the Pentagon budget has served as industrial and regional development policies for over 40 years. How these formerly favored precincts will be affected by the military "build-down" remains to be seen. Although current policies may be reversed – as new threats in the post-Cold War world are discovered and the American political economy finds it cannot live with demobilization.

Sources to the map:
Saunders, Norman C. "Employment Effects of the Rise and Fall in Defense Spending." *Monthly Labor Review*, no.116: 4 (April 1993): 3-11; U.S. Bureau of the Census. *Statistical Abstract of the United States: 1993*. Washington, D.C., 1993; U.S. Department of Defense. *Worldwide List of Military Installations*. Washington, D.C., 1992; U.S Department of Defense. "Aspin Forwards Recommendations to Base Closure Commission." *News Release* 101-93 (12 March 1993) Washington, D.C., 1993; U.S Department of Defense. "More U.S. Overseas Bases to End Operations." *News Release* 298-93 (1 July 1993). Washington, D.C., 1993; U.N. Development Program. *Human Development Report 1993*. New York: Oxford University Press, 1993.